The Yakovlev Yak-1 Family

In Profile & Scale

Erik Pilawskii

Contents

Introduction   1
I-26 and Yak-1 Profiles   2-35
A Brief Examination of I-26 & Yak-1 Development   36-40
Scale Line Drawings   41-99
Glossary & Abbreviations   100
Transliteration Guide   101
Recommended Reading   101
Appendix I: Yak-1 Camouflage & Colouration   102-104
Appendix II: Yak-1 № 08-68 'UA'   105
Appendix III: Yak-1 Stabiliser Development   106
Appendix IV: Yak-1B № 08-110   107

RED BANNER
AVIATION
RESEARCH · ARTWORK · PUBLICATION
WWW.REDBANNER.CO.UK

First Published 2019
ISBN 978-0-244-47532-1
Second Edition

Aleksandr Yakovlev's I-26 design-- which in time would blossom into the **Yak-1 family**-- arrived at a moment of great changes within Soviet aviation. Three separate fighter designs had been accepted during 1939 to modernise the VVS inventory, each with their own interesting and purposeful features. Of these-- the I-301, the I-200 and the I-26-- it was the Yakovlev machine which was the most conventional, and yet simultaneously also the most inspired. A virtual committee of designers had sculpted the I-301, making use of radical new wood-plastics and other construction materials, while the I-200 was conceived as a high-altitude interceptor. But, the I-26 was a classic Yak OKB design, differing little from the tried and tested structural techniques used in previous aircraft from the bureau. The innovations in the design were of an aerodynamic order, not one of construction methodology nor materials.

It was this very aerodynamic refinement of the aircraft which was its genius. Even the prototype I-26s-- and more so the mature Yak fighters-- demonstrated outstanding handling and behaviour. Indeed, not only was the aircraft highly responsive and manoeuvrable, but simultaneously possessed of safe and predictable flight characteristics suitable for inexperienced pilots. So much so, in fact, that the design was immediately adopted as a training machine, virtually unchanged. In combat, this delightful handling proved to be a tremendous asset, both nurturing neophyte airmen into seasoned veterans, but also permitting experienced pilots to push the machine bitterly hard, to the *absolute* limit, and thereby gain those tiny advantages in battle which could tip the scales in their favour. Of all Soviet aces of the Great Patriotic War, it is little wonder that the majority of them flew Yakovlev's fighters.

This, then, is the colourful and fascinating story of the Yak-1 Family, ***In Profile and Scale...***

The I-26

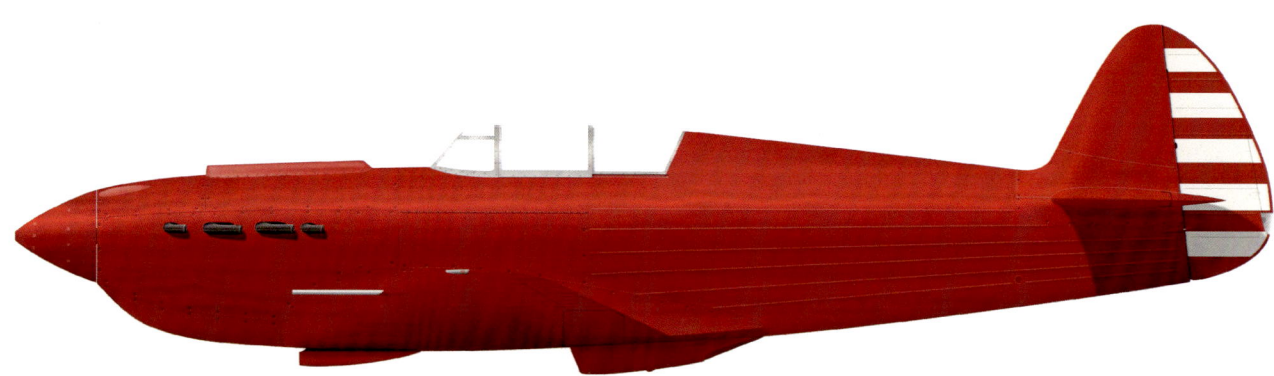

When the glossy red Prototype № 1 first took to the air on 13 January 1940, Senior Engineer Adler remarked that it was as if, "A bright red jewel had slipped into the sky, dazzling everyone". The exact red paint used by the OKB is not known, but the finish was indeed gloss and applied over the entire airframe. Tragically, Pilot-Engineer Piontkovskii lost his life in this very machine on 27 April. Three subsequent crash investigations determined that the prototype's structure was insufficiently stressed, but despite all efforts, could not agree with certainty as to what caused the catastrophe. Sudden excessive wing loading due to the gear's unexpected deployment and failure of the wing outer structure to sympathetic vibration were the leading explanations, but no definitive conclusion was ever reached. The No 2 prototype was initially painted identically to the № 1, but subsequently re-finished with a more 'military' scheme following airframe strengthening modifications later in the summer.

Moscow built I-26 example p/n 0209 came down heavily on 31 October 1940 during factory flight testing. An engine failure at low altitude forced test pilot Plygoonov to set down roughly, whereupon the port gear collapsed. Like most Moscow built examples, 0209 was finished with a dark, gloss paint, and surely one suspects that this must be lacquer AEh-15, long known to be a favourite finish of several Moscow facilities (such as Factory № 1, № 39, etc).

"White 16" was Moscow built I-26 p/n 0406, here seen under investigation at the NII VVS, October 1940. The finish was again dark and glossy, and must have been AEh-15 Dark Green. National red star insignia look not to have been applied to the fin/rudder on most I-26 examples for reasons unknown, neither in Moscow nor Saratov. The rather aft placement of the fuselage star was typical for Factory № 301 I-26s.

Saratov built Series 3 example p/n 05-03 is shown in a photograph taken by German forces, presumably during the summer of 1941. Like so many early I-26s, it uncertain whether this aircraft was actually operating in active service, or was simply abandoned due to the teething problems common in such examples. No tactical number can be seen, and the fin/rudder is lacking any national insignia.

"White 10" was the long serving Moscow built I-26 p/n 0610. This machine soldiered on with the 21 IAP-KBF until August 1942, which might be something of a record for I-26s remaining in active service. The fuselage star placement and lack of insignia on the fin/rudder suggest that this was the original factory livery, but clearly in this case not AEh-15 lacquer.

The Yak-1, Early Saratov Examples

The much photographed Yak-1 p/n 05-11, which was delivered to Moscow for State testing during July 1941. Even the earliest examples of proper "Yak-1s" (from Series 9) from Saratov wore a two-colour camouflage upper surface scheme with Black over Green. This pattern was virtually identical to another such simplified pattern used during MiG-3 manufacture at the same time. 05-11 lacks a fin star marking and tactical number, but features a delicate red tip to the spinner.

"White 3" of the 123 IAP, near Moscow, autumn 1941. This example is a bit of a mystery in that it seems to have a single colour upper surface finish, and not a camouflage scheme. The undersurfaces are not in view (the aircraft is shown having crash-landed), and so the exact Series of the machine cannot be determined. There have been suggestions that this aircraft was one of the 65 Factory No 30 examples, and while possible the author believes that "3" was more likely from Saratov Series 9-11.

Yak-1 p/n 14-13 was seen, background, in a rather poor image derived from a 16 mm cine still taken during the winter of 1941 at the 236 IAP. Alas, several pilots are standing in front of the rudder, and it cannot be determined if the tactical number was "White 1" (as shown), or included a second digit. The finish is classic for early Saratov machines, while the number was clearly applied at the so-called 'ground angle'.

The *utterly* spectacular early Yak-1 of HSU Georgi N. Zhidov, 123 IAP, winter 1941. In fact, Zhidov's aircraft was the original 'Yak-1', a Series 9 (Saratov built) example sporting some interesting field applied modifications and details. Unusually for its age, this machine was indeed fitted with an RSI-4 radio set and accompanying stub dipole and aerial. The main sliding canopy was removed altogether, a modification favoured by some of the longer serving VVS pilots (such as Vorozheikin and Bobrov). Four RO132 rocket rails were installed under the wings-- which in fact was the preferred arrangement when adding such armament in the field (as opposed to six RO82 rails)-- with four RS-82 missiles in view. Lastly, the port side ammunition tray cover had been replaced with a somewhat ill fitting unit taken from a Moscow built I-26 example, of which several had served with the regiment. "Red 23" shows the unmistakable effects of several bouts of repainting and finishing. It would appear that MK-7 White had been applied over the entire upper surface at some point, then later this finish partly removed (as happened when the pilots discovered the dire drag penalties this paint imposed), and thereafter covered up by a dapple of appliqué over the rear part of the airframe. It is impossible to know which part of the underlying camouflage, if any, was original to the aircraft when built.

Georgii Nikonorovich Zhidov

Official Score: 13 + 13
Missions: 366

Claims While Flying The Yak-1: 12 + 9

The Yak-1, *Massovii* Examples

One of a number of early *massovii* Yak-1s in service with the 8 IAP VVS-ChF appearing in a famous series of images taken during the spring of 1942. "White 5", "6", "8" and "9" are all known in this group of photos. It has been suggested that this aircraft belonged to regimental commander L. K. Votolkin, but at the time of writing the author is aware of no confirmation of this attribution.

HSU Mikhail V. Avdeev's original Yak-1 fighter, "White 5" of the 8 IAP VVS-ChF, 1942. It was in this trusty machine that Avdeev rose to prominence following his participation in the heroic defence of Sevastopol'. As an *eskadrilya* commander Avdeev won the unstinting admiration of his pilots, showing himself committed to the improvement of the unit above all else and eschewing personal glory or recognition. Indeed, he was said to routinely assign his own claims to other pilots in the *eskadrilya*, or even to fail to claim them at all. Modest and long in VVS service after the war, Avdeedv himself never wrote about his wartime successes, nor attempted to redress his official tally of "12 + 6" Confirmed claims, which the pilots of his regiments regarded as both insulting and laughable.

Another superb portrait shot of Avdeev by eminent Soviet photographer E.F. Khaldei. A charming Khaldei photo of Avdeev is also known with his daughter, who is holding a duck!

Mikhail Vasil'evich Avdeev

OFFICIAL SCORE: 12 + 6
MISSIONS: ~400

Claims While Flying The Yak-1: 7 + 5

▲ Yet another Avdeev Yak-1 bearing the tactical number '5', this example, "Red 5" was photographed during the early winter months of 1942-43. Promoted during the summer to commander of the 6 GvIAP-ChF, and awarded the Gold Star Hero of the Soviet Union (№ 858), Avdeev seems to have started his wartime habit of decorating the tail of his aircraft with 'claim stars' on this machine. "Red 5" was freshly turned out in the image, sporting a fine MK-7 White finish and a black spinner. It is thought that his personal tally of 10 victories was replicated on both sides of the fin/rudder.

"Red 26" was photographed by German forces having crash landed in fairly good order, date and location unknown. The aircraft was finished with a well executed MK-7 winter upper surface, but the national star markings were rather small for factory application and might have been applied at the unit. The tactical numeral was completed in a very attractive and somewhat large font. Interestingly, this machine was fitted with a three-piece spinner from an LaGG-3 fighter.

One of a sizeable number of still images taken from some classic 16 mm *cine* stock of Yak fighters at the front during the spring of 1942 distributed by TASS during the war. "Red 34", seen foreground, was a rocket-armed aircraft of the Series 43-48 range, and retains its longer Hucks collar and spinner, as built. its winter finish is mostly intact, and the main gear's lower door cover has been removed, as was occasionally done when operating in muddy conditions. The unit in operation is thought to be the 238 IAP on the Leningrad front.

Dramatic footage of Yak-1 fighters taxiing out over the frosty ground of a spring morning. The relative quality of this film sequence cannot be over-stated: the lighting condition were diabolical, and additionally the photographer had to deal with ice and water vapour spraying about wildly! Despite all difficulties, the film images were outstanding. The camera operator must have been a professional of the *absolute* highest calibre.

▼ "Red 85" from the same TASS sequence. This example was a later model than "34", but still rocket armed and also lacking a radio set. The winter finish was somewhat worn, and interestingly had been removed over part of the fuselage and tail. The extensive exhaust staining is testament to the hard fighting of the winter of 1941-42.

HSU P. I. Pavlov of the 21 IAP-KBF taxiing out in his Yak-1 "White 5" p/n 11-55, summer 1942. Once mis-identified by this author as a factory camouflage scheme, this example in fact demonstrates one of a species of widely seen field applications, these used to replace the winter MK-7 White finish with which they were built. The colouration is not provably known, and the disruptive colour would usually be expected to have been AMT-6 Black. However, the appearance of the subject does not appear to be this lacquer in the eyes of the author, and AII Dk. Green has been used in the profile [above]. Readers may decide for themselves which is the more likely option.

A TASS supplied image of "White 23" and associated pilots, presumably during the spring of 1942 (Second Battle of Kharkov). The name of the regimental commander is tantalisingly unreadable.

"White 23" was subject of yet another widely circulated TASS wartime shot, and indeed this image was even reproduced in Life magazine. Such hard-edged colour demarcations are the stuff of field camouflage, and one suspect that this is what we see here, despite the admitted similarity to certain factory schemes. Alas, the unit and commander's name have been obliterated in the scan supplied to the author, and for now the correct attribution of this example remains unknown.

Two Yak-1s preparing for a flight, date and location unknown. "White 21", foreground, is a very late M-105PF powered example of Series 90-98. This aircraft was finished in AMT lacquers -4/-6/-7 as suitable for the timing of its manufacture. Fortuitously, this finish may be contrasted directly on the same image with an earlier machine painted in AII style lacquers Green/Lt. Blue/Black on "White 34". Note the darker appearance of AMT-4 Green vs AII Green, and also of AII Lt. Blue vs AMT-7. A white spinner completes a classic late-model Yak-1 scheme.

This rather handsome example may be seen behind "White 21" in the same image [above]. The camouflage application and details are absolutely classic for an example of the Series 65-80 range, and one feels certain that is what we have here. The spinner shows a lovely red and white trim, and similarly the rudder trim tab has been picked out in the former colour.

"White 2" was photographed by German forces having crash landed on a snowy field, date unknown. A light 'dusting' of winter MK-7 white was seen along the fuselage and wings in a manner more reminiscent of such partial winter schemes seen around Stalingrad the following year. Rocket rails were fitted to this example but no radio set nor mast.

"White 21" is a fascinating example for many reasons. The aircraft wears a field applied scheme using AMT-4 and -6 lacquers with an odd disruptive pattern of angular lines and shapes and hard-edged demarcations. The lower surfaces, however, appear to remain finished as built with AII Lt. Blue paint. These 'mixed' schemes must have been fairly common, surprisingly, as they were in fact suggested by the Government as an officially recommended procedure. [see Appendix I] A longer style Hucks collar was fitted, and no radio mast was present.

▼ It is a rare case when wartime aircraft are documented from both sides in the photographic record, but happily "Red 37" is just such an example. When photographed by German forces the aircraft was in a somewhat derelict state, and the following profiles depict the machine as it would have been at the time of its loss. A field applied camouflage largely approximating factory patternation was seen, and both the numerals and national insignia were boldly trimmed with white. Rocket rails, a larger Hucks starter collar and a paint-free canopy details are all in view.

The much photographed personal Yak-1 fighter of Hero of the Soviet Union M.D. Baranov, "White 1", autumn 1942. By the time of the Stalingrad campaign Baranov was already a well known public figure, one of the great early leaders within Soviet wartime aviation, akin to men like Safonov and Golubev. Despite a boyish demeanour and toothy grin, Baranov was utterly fearless, and was known to press home attacks to the closest range. Indeed, on 6th August, while defending Il-2s from attack, and having already dispatched two Bf 109s and a Ju 87, he ran out of ammunition chasing yet another enemy fighter, whereupon Baranov rammed it to destruction. In this *taran* attack he was himself wounded and taken to hospital, returning to active service in December. Alas, Baranov was tragically lost in a flight accident on 17 January 1943 when his fighter crashed while giving low-level combat instruction to a novice pilot. For reasons unknown his Army official score is highly abbreviated-- only 24 Personal claims-- and none of his 28 Shared claims are mentioned at all.

The inscription, applied to both port and starboard, reads, *"Groza Fashistov M.D. Baranov"* [Warning Fascists It's M.D. Baranov]. It is hard to imagine a more suitable text.

Mikhail Dmitrievich Baranov

OFFICIAL SCORE: 24
MISSIONS: ~200

Claims While Flying The Yak-1: 20

"White 1" shows evidence of very considerable re-painting, as befitting a heavily used combat example. On balance, the upper finish in view seems to have been completed with AMT lacquers, but quite possibly when built this aircraft wore the earlier AII variety. Indeed, the undersurface colour is a bit more suggestive of AII Light Blue than AMT-7 in the author's eyes, but the profiles [above and below] depict AMT paints throughout.

This attractive Yak-1 p/n 03-43 was photographed with the pilot-- a despicable defector to Fascist Germany-- clearly in view at the tail. The three-digit tactical numeral, "Red 201", was not entirely uncommon, being something of a fad in certain regiments. The aircraft looks to have been quite new when handed over to the enemy intact, and demonstrated the various details of its Series' manufacture. Most likely this pilot later met the same fate as the majority of Russian defectors-- they were murdered by their erstwhile Nazi 'friends'.

Ekaterina Vasil'eva Budanova

OFFICIAL SCORE: 6 + 5
MISSIONS: 266

Claims While Flying The Yak-1: 6 + 5

Heroine of the Russian Federation E. V. Budannova's Yak-1 p/n 44-92 with the 758 IAP, late 1942. For too long this machine was misidentified as having belonged to HSU Litvyak, but indeed it did not. This idea is a bit of an error of modern prejudice, in fact; one should recall that at the time of this photo (and the related series published by TASS outlets) that Budanova was by far more popular in the public eye than the then unknown Litvyak. "White 44" was a late model Yak-1 of Series 92 and would have been fitted with the M-105PF engine and other related version details [see Scale Line Drawings p.82].

"White 2" was a very late model Yak-1 of Series 90-98, but whose ownership is currently unknown. The scheme is a somewhat curious field application using AMT lacquers, and the national star insignia have not been applied with great care, suggesting a complete re-finish job. This aircraft also highlights a rather strange curiosity with respect to VVS markings habits, in that many Yak-1s during 1942 demonstrate single digit tactical numbers. Such single numbers were not common on other aircraft at this time. One wonders why their use would have been something of a fad within Yak operating regiments of the period, but not others?

Yak-1 p/n 10-45 photographed in service with the 21 *Aviapolk* of the VVS-KBF, date unknown. The aircraft wears a worn winter MK-7 application with a smartly painted rudder trim tab. Curiously, despite the significant score displayed on the fuselage, the pilot of this aircraft is not currently known. No tactical number is in view, but a larger Hucks collar may be seen on this example.

"White 31" is another attractive late model Yak-1 demonstrating a field applied camouflage finish of curious detail. As with nearly all such work, AMT lacquers have been applied, but the angular lines of the scheme are unique. A lovely trimmed band adorns the fin/rudder, and on balance this would seem to be red in colour. Many profiles exist of this aircraft showing alternate colour interpretations, and it must be admitted that a blue shade similar to A-10 primer would fit the tone and contrast of the image [see inset, left]. Be that as it may, the author suspects that the item is red, and certainly the more 'creative' renditions of this device may be ignored.

Technicians servicing "White 31" along the Stalingrad Front region, 1942.

"White 27" was the personal mount of HSU E. V. Petrenko, autumn 1942. Then a *Starshii Leitenant* in command of the 20 IAP-SF's 2nd *Eskadrilya*, Petrenko's Yak shows nine claim stars applied to the fin. The camouflage scheme is unusual, but also well completed, and it is unclear whether this was a factory or field application. A white spinner and tail flash complete this attractive late model example of Series 90-98 manufacture. Petrenko would go on to command the 20 IAP-SF and finished the war with an official tally of 13 + 3 Confirmed victories.

The Yak-1, Winterised Examples

"White 6" was photographed on a snowy aerodrome awaiting take-off during the Battle of Moscow. The sight of a temperate camouflaged aircraft with ski gear seems contradictory, but quite in fact a number of machines served throughout the battle in exactly this kind of colouration. "White 6" was an example of the pre-*massovii* winterised aircraft built during September and October, 1941.

"White 15" featured in a series of well published photographs showing early ski-equipped Yaks near Moscow, exact date and unit unknown. Most RO rocket rails were left unpainted, or were finished in the undersurface camouflage colour (e.g. AII Light Blue), but in some cases these were painted with a black finish. "White 15" is a good example of this practice, and one wonders what the purpose of this behaviour might have been?

"Red 18" featured a fairly worn winter finish and was photographed in service with PVO forces around Moscow, early 1942. Curiously, the fuselage star marking had been painted around, but the tail star was seems not to have been, suggesting that it was re-applied entirely.

One of the great, enduring Yak colouration mysteries is this winterised example which was photographed by German forces during 1942. Even though the aircraft has been heavily stripped by souvenir hunters, the original finish is still largely in view. The mystery finish was carefully applied over-all (e.g. upper and lower surfaces), and features a rather reflective surface. Indeed, it matches in many ways the reflective properties of the dural engine bay framing and fuselage steel tube structure. Therefore, the author concludes that the most likely explanation is that this machine was re-painted with an over-all AII Aluminium scheme. If true, this would not be the only such example on a modern fighter: at least one LaGG-3 is known in such a finish, along with several Naval P-39s. In any event, a Yak-1 with a bright, reflective silvery finish makes for a *most* handsome appearance.

Venerable old "Blue 9" is a remarkable example in terms of Soviet period aircraft marking practices. When photos of this machine were first published in the 1960s, it set off a 'storm' of spurious colour profiles of various VVS subjects featuring numbers inside of national star insignia. Indeed, virtually all types of aircraft were depicted in this way. However, and of course, these were all erroneous. This example, "Blue 9", is the only specimen known to the author to feature tactical numerals carefully positioned inside of the national markings (field applied numbers covering or superimposed onto such stars are known, of course) in such a manner. Equally, the use of a blue paint (here rendered with A-9 primer) was unique, and also carefully chosen by the artist to compliment its suitably restrained contrast to the red star. This example was built between Series 55 and 65, with all relevant version details clearly in view [see Scale Line Drawings, p.76].

The famous and well photographed Yak-1 p/n 38-55 at the NII VVS for examination, winter 1941. This aircraft served as the production example (the so-called *etalon*) for the series winterised model, and as a Series 55 aircraft it was fitted with six RO82 rocket rails. The upper profile shows these items removed so as to highlight a very odd phenomenon which affected machines under evaluation by the testing fraternities (both the NII VVS and the LII). It was extremely common that whenever either institute was required (or inclined) to apply national insignia, they did so in a disastrous manner which defies understanding. How two such august institutions-- world leaders in scientific and aerodynamic study-- could descend into slap-stick incompetence when introduced to a paint tin remains incomprehensible, but such examples are utterly ubiquitous in the photographic record.

In this case, application of the underside star was required after the lower wings were experimentally painted white outboard of the central fuselage. This idea was no doubt inspired by certain MiG-3 aircraft, whose outer wing undersurfaces were finished in this way. It remains unclear if such a scheme was ever applied to winterised Yaks at the factory, but at least one unidentifiable aircraft was photographed at the LII finished entirely in MK-7 White, upper and lower surfaces.

The Yak-1B, Early Examples

"White 2" demonstrates a quite interesting, and one must say fairly well executed, field applied camouflage using the current lacquers AMT-4 Green and -6 Black. The plethora of quirky and, at times, appalling ad-hoc camouflage seen on Yak-1s during 1943 resulted from the fact that Factory № 292 *did not* follow the specific instructions given to them in this regard. A full temperate scheme was to have been applied at the factory before the winter MK-7 White coat was added, and as one may see in the photographic record, this was rarely done (or indeed, not at all). The fuselage national star on "2" has been outlined thinly with black.

"Red 5" is the subject of a now very widely published photograph, but alas the ownership of this colourful machine remains unknown. Two white tactical bands are in view, along with white trim on the canopy, and a somewhat worn red nose. The inscription is a dedication from the workers of the Pugachevskii region, and ten claim stars can be seen. The star on the fin/rudder has been trimmed in white.

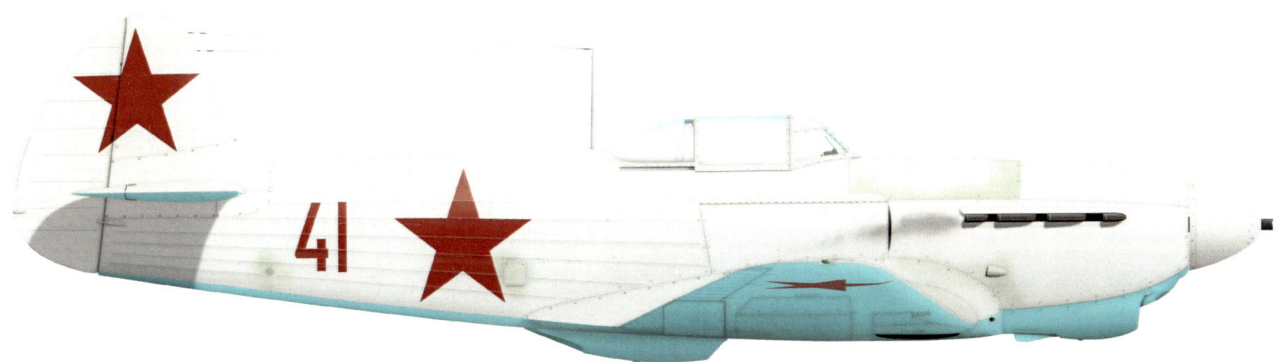

"Red 41" sported a fairly well kept winter finish, but with areas of wear evident over the wing root and cowling. The appearance of this example must have been absolutely typical for Yak-1 operations during the early spring of 1943.

Starshii Lt. Viktor F. Korobov of the 34 IAP was photographed along with his Yak-1B "Red 8" on 28 August 1943. This aircraft wears a nice AMT-4/-6 scheme, complete with black trimmed national stars and also trim around the number "8". Nine claim stars can be seen along the turtle-decking, and these seem to have been rendered quite professionally. Korobov's official score at the war's end is given as 9 + 8 Confirmed victories.

This wonderful winter camouflage example, "Red 4", was the personal mount of HSU Vasilii I. Shishkin, then of the 581 IAP, early 1943. Shishkin received his first Yak-1 bearing this same dedication text (from the "*Signal Revolutsii*" collective farm) at the Saratov factory, and there are known photos of him in the cockpit greeting the collective's farmers. That aircraft wore temperate camouflage, and the font style of the dedication text was rather different. Shishkin retained this aircraft-- thought to be p/n 34-104-- through 1943, and it later demonstrated the same text and style in white on its AMT-4/-6 temperate camouflage. The red spinner and flash make for a quite stunning appearance.

Vasilii Ivanovich Shishkin

OFFICIAL SCORE: 12 + 16
MISSIONS: 541

Claims While Flying The Yak-1: 10 + 11

"Red 100" somewhere at the Kursk salient front, 1943. The appearance of a T-34 tank, background, is highly apropos to these details. The aircraft wore a curious field applied scheme (AMT lacquers), and shows signs of multiple episodes of repainting. The pattern over the cowling is obviously a reconstruction, as the unit is not in view.

The delightful Yak-1B of Yakov N, Kutikhin, 247 IAP, autumn 1943. Kutikhin flew at least two highly personalised Yak-1B aircraft, and alas the details of both have become somewhat inter-mixed and confused. This early model, finished in an AMT-4/-6/-7 scheme, was "White 47", with the tactical number appearing on the port fuselage. The number to starboard was obliterated and replaced by this sea eagle artwork which, it must be pointed out, was superbly rendered by a proper artist and not by some amateur hack (such as the author!). The colouration of the eagle artwork can only be guessed at, of course. The national star markings were delightfully trimmed in white, and a large arrow feature was painted on the fuselage (it is thought on both sides). Kutikhin is seen in front of another, later Yak-1B, this example finished in AMT-11/-12/7 and wearing a Guard's emblem on the port nose (which "47" did not have) as suitable for his service within the 12 GvIAD command. This later machine is *suspected* to have been "White 34", but at the time of writing the author is not yet convinced of this detail.

The Yak-1B, *Massovii* Examples

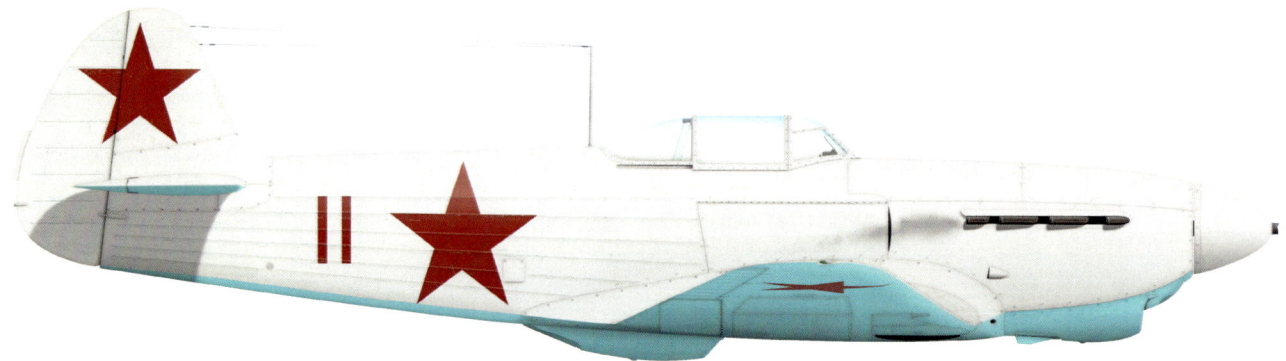

This wonderfully turned out example-- indeed, virtually spotless-- *must* have been photographed at the factory (by E.F. Khaldei, no less) early in 1943. The finish and details of "Red 11" are prototypical for early Yak-1B manufacture, and this aircraft must have been one of the very last completed in an MK-7 White winter scheme.

▲ ▼ These two examples are seen in an extensive series of images of freshly delivered Yak-1Bs at a naval regiment of the KBF, 1943. Numbers "24", "27", "34", "43", "44" and "47" are all known, and are virtually identical in appearance. The white rudder and spinner were a classic Baltic Fleet device, used in a way as a *de facto* identification marking.

Lidiya Vladimirovna Litvyak

OFFICIAL SCORE: 4 + 3
MISSIONS: ~150

Claims While Flying The Yak-1: 4 + 3

Following a major revision of all known Litvyak photographic material, the author has completed this new and slightly modified profile of her Yak-1B "White 23". A recently published image shows the 'scrubbed out' area which Litvyak herself mentions, where she had removed the six 'claim stars' below the cockpit and replaced them with white lilies. This same view gives a bit more evidence about the pattern of her field applied camouflage scheme, as well. There remains, sadly, no available information regarding the starboard side appearance of this aircraft.

The famous and much discussed Yak-1B of HSU Sergei Luganskii, "White 58". The exact timing of this well published series of images showing the machine with Luganskii are still a matter of debate, and on balance the author feels that sometime in 1945 is the most likely (but not post-war). The NKAP style camouflage is quite generic; it could be either a factory or better quality field application. A white tactical band was seen over the rear fuselage, and an exceedingly delightful trimmed star on the spinner. Many colour permutations have been mooted for the wreath object, and the author is unimpressed by all of them-- it surely was white in colour. Equally, the oft replicated white flash on the rudder is also not supported by any evidence in the author's view.

Sergei Danilovich Luganskii

OFFICIAL SCORE: 37 + 5
MISSIONS: 390

Claims While Flying The Yak-1: 34 + 3

Without doubt a rather poor image, nevertheless this photograph of a Yak-1B line-up at an unknown regiment (possibly the 866 IAP) shows us some superb examples. "White 41" bears the dedication text, "Liberated Donbass", in a very fine script. The white flash on the rudder is a tactical marking, obviously in use widely in the regiment. Despite the date-- likely spring 1944-- this example still retains its older AMT-4/-6 upper surface colouration.

▼ "White 40", foreground, showing the regimental tactical flash on the rudder as well as a fine red stripe. The scheme is a field applied NKAP style finish in AMT-11/-12/7 colours, as suitable for the date. The red spinner demonstrated a superb trimmed star on the tip.

▼ "White 02" also sported an AMT-11/-12/7 field scheme, this with curious 'ramp' features and undersurface colour on the rudder. The rudder flash has been embellished with broad white stripes and tip, and the white spinner is adorned with a lovely red star.

HSU A. V. Alelyukhin is well remembered for his famous La-7 fighter, "White 14", but in fact the majority of his victories were scored flying the Yak-1, including this handsome -1B model, "Red 1". Many profiles of this machine depict the heart emblem to be in red colour, but surely this is incorrect-- it was without doubt white. The 'pouncing tiger' was a personal device, and painted on the aircraft with some skill. The red spinner is a bit of speculation, based on Alelyukhin's own comments, and there is no currently known photographic evidence covering this detail.

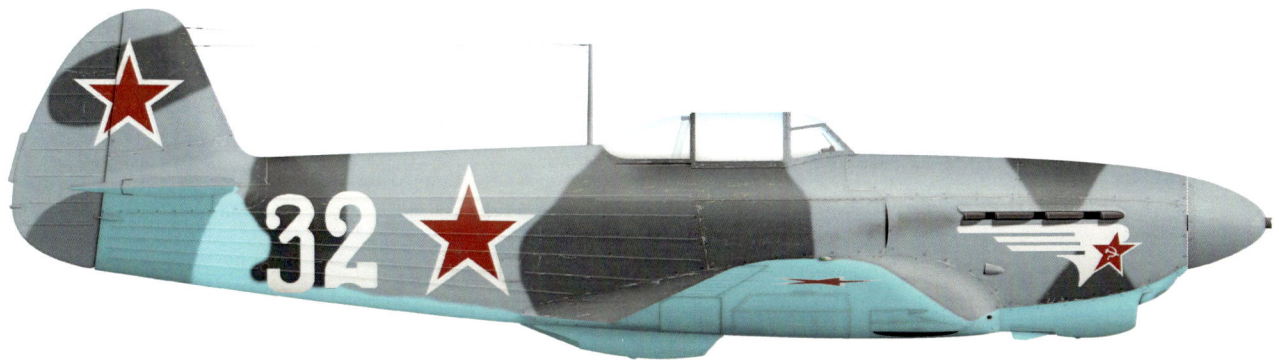

"White 32" was photographed in service with an as yet undetermined regiment within the 3 IAK, 1944. This Corps' emblem, the 'winged star', was *superbly* executed on the nose of this machine in the 'normal' manner; that is to say, in white with a red star. As fine as the nose artwork was, the tactical number "32" was equally poor and out-of-sorts, and one wonders if this amateurish appearance resulted from some kind of local re-painting?

One regiment within the 3 IAK, the 812 IAP, was noted for applying a 'reversed' Corps badge onto their Yak-1Bs. "White 2" is just such an example, seen here at the time it fell into enemy hands (where it was subsequently re-painted and tested). To accommodate the red 'wings' then entire 'chin' was sometimes painted in white, as on this machine. The small dedication text on the fuselage was from the workers of the Frunzenskii region to pilot Leonid Smirnov. The finish looks to have been a field applied AMT-4/-6 example of slightly odd detail.

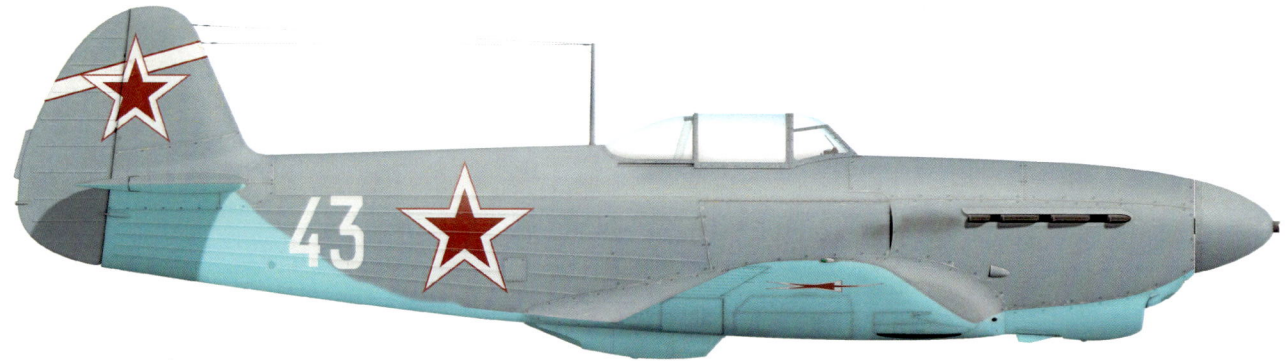

With the pilot stood proudly in the cockpit, this finely turned out Yak-1B, "White 43", was likely photographed just after the end of the war. The conspicuous lack of wear and tear, the single-colour AMT-11 finish and post-war regulation sized out-line ("Victory" type) national insignia are a tell-tale give-away as to the timing of the shot. A neatly trimmed flash on the fin/rudder adds to this handsome scheme.

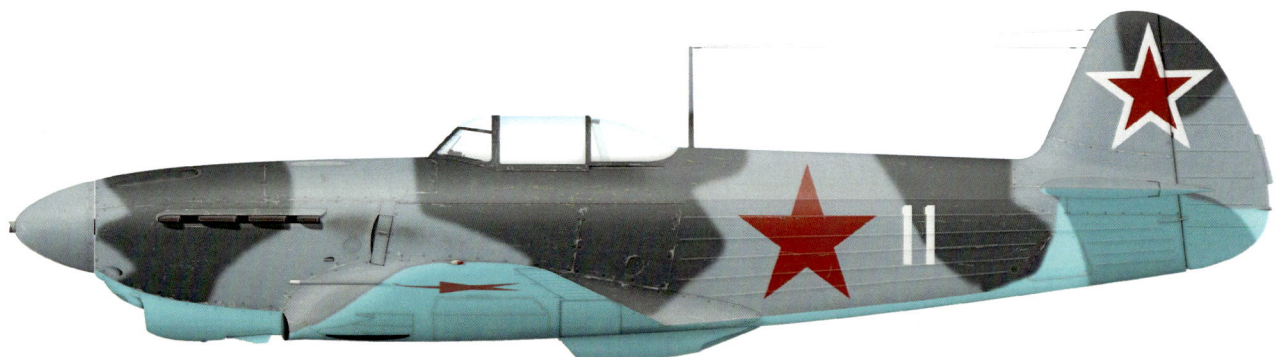

"White 11" was photographed in service with the № 1 Polish Regiment "*Warszawa*" during the summer of 1944. The scheme is clearly a field applied NKAP style finish with curiously angular lines. The use of a plain red star on the fuselage is odd, and perhaps points to yet additional local repainting? Despite being rather irregular, one is compelled to admit that the over-all appearance of "11" is quite appealing.

"White 45", allegedly of the 153 GvIAP, was photographed in a series of images showing numerous Yak-1Bs of essentially the same appearance. Indeed, so prototypical is the this aircraft's NKAP style finish, tactical number style and other details that it might stand for a whole generation of 1944 Saratov production.

HSU Boris N. Eremin flew a number of Yak-1 aircraft, and it would seem that all of his Yak-1B machines bore the same inscription (a dedication from collective farm foreman F. Golovatii). Indeed, there are a startling number of photos of Eremin sitting in aircraft so marked, some with a white MK-7 finish, and others in AMT-4/-6 temperate schemes. This aircraft-- seen above (profile) and below right-- is none of those. In fact, this is Yak-1B p/n 08-110 which had been used at the Factory № 292 workshops for various testing purposes, and which was subsequently decorated after the war to depict Eremin's aircraft and put on display in Saratov. Even so, it bore at least two different renditions of this dedication text while so displayed (the profile showing an earlier version, and the photo a later one), and possibly yet more appearances besides (see below). [See Appendix IV for a discussion of 08-110]

Boris Nikolaievich Eremin
[Ерёмин]

OFFICIAL SCORE: 8 + 15
MISSIONS: 342

Claims While Flying The Yak-1: 8 + 15

[Left] For a variety of reasons, a significant number of Soviet pilots experienced difficulties with the Air Force Command's subsequent post-war reckoning of claims and Official scores. B N Eremin is a classic case in point. A hugely decorated pilot of great experience, and with over three hundred combat missions, his own estimation of his personal score was some 30 enemy aircraft. His official tally remains 8 Personal and 15 Shared Confirmed victories, all from his service in the Yak-1.

Yak-1B p/n 08-110 on display in Saratov, 1945.

▼ Eremin in the cockpit of one of his winter scheme Yak-1Bs. The dedication text in these cases was in red, and it made for a very attractive appearance indeed. Alas, and almost unbelievably given the number of such photographs, there exists not enough evidence of the remainder of any of these aircraft so as to execute an accurate colour profile! What is the tactical number, how are the national insignia arranged, what of other details? Incredibly, we just do not now know.

[Right] Yet another Eremin Yak-1B with his 'Golovatii' inscription. This machine is finished in lacquers AMT-11/-12, which is a curiosity as Eremin is not known to have flown such a Yak-1. From the autumn of 1944 he flew a Yak-3 in this colouration with a different style of inscription (same text), but aside from this image, always in earlier finishes. Moreover, this aircraft wears a remarkable "reversed" star marking of a *white* insignia with *red* trim. Such an item might be fine for artistic purposes, but certainly it would not be suitable for military service. On that basis, could this aircraft be yet another replacement dedication aircraft, or even 08-110 in yet a different guise?

27

Aleksei Mikhailovich Reshetov

OFFICIAL SCORE: 35 + 8
MISSIONS: ~800

Claims While Flying The Yak-1: 18 + 6

One of the great Yak aces of the GPW, HSU Aleksei M. Reshetov was initially known for his prowess in the Yak-7, and was widely photographed in front of such aircraft. This attractive Yak-1B, "White 16", dates from Reshetov's service in the 31 GvIAP during the autumn of 1944. The delightful dedication text is from the *Shotovskii* Collective Farm, rendered in white. The scheme was a typical NKAP style application, this with suggestions of some local re-touching. Many profiles exist of this machine showing a star painted on the spinner, but the author is aware of no evidence supporting this feature.

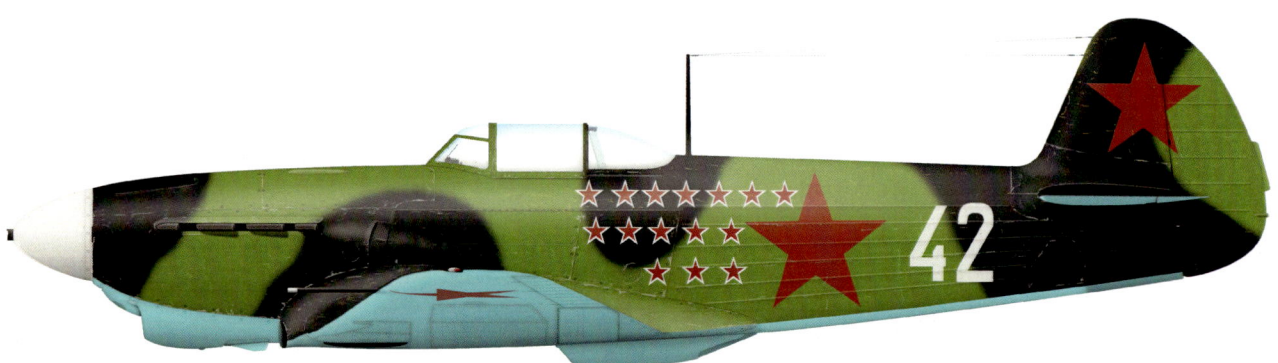

"White 42" was the very attractive Yak-1B of HSU Nikolai A. Kozlov, 910 IAP, 1943. Hugely experienced, Kozlov flew a remarkable number of different fighters-- to include the I-16, MiG-3, Yak-1, Yak-7, La-5 and La-7-- and indeed scored in most of them. "White 42" featured an unusual AMT-4/-6 scheme (of unknown origin) with 15 claim stars beautifully painted on the fuselage, and a white spinner.

Nikolai Aleksandrovich Kozlov

OFFICIAL SCORE: 16 + 7
MISSIONS: 620

Claims While Flying The Yak-1: 8 + 2

HSU Vladimir P. Pokrovskii of the Northern Fleet was another favourite-- and much photographed-- subject of photographer E. F. Khaldei. Pokrovskii was a notable Kittyhawk ace, and his well known Yak-1B (above) dates from his time in command of the 2 GvIAP-SF, ca. autumn 1944. One may only lament that the various images of this aircraft were not shot by Khaldei, as they are quite poor in quality and leave much to interpret. An entire article covering this example may be found on the author's web site, and readers are recommended to follow the QR Code link [right] to this for additional reading and discussion. The profile here shows the author's preferred interpretation of the scheme with an AMT-12 rear fuselage and gold-trimmed claim stars.

Vladimir Pavlovich Pokrovskii

OFFICIAL SCORE: 12 + 6
MISSIONS: 340

Claims While Flying The Yak-1: none known

Fotii Yakovlevich Morozov

OFFICIAL SCORE: 16 + 5
MISSIONS: 857

Claims While Flying The Yak-1: 9 + 4

Hugely famous, iterations and interpretations of HSU Morozov's Yak-1B "White 50" abound. The artwork was indeed spectacular, and one suspects that the two elements were not applied at the same time nor by the same hand. The snake over the tail was highly creative in execution, but the liberation of Poland artwork forward of this was expertly painted; certainly by no amateur. The finish was a classic NKAP type with white bordered national markings as suitable for the timing of the image (summer 1944).

Fotii Ya. Morozov in front of his wonderfully painted Yak-1B "White 50", 31 GvIAP, 1944. The regiment boasted some of the finest Yak aces of the entire war.

"White 22" was a *massovii oblehchennyi* Yak-1B model which served with the 53 GvIAP during the late summer of 1943. The various *oblegchennyi* details were evident in the image, including a metal fin, Yak-3 style stabilisers, blanked off UBS and so forth. The scheme was a late appearing AMT-4/-6/-7 application, and could well have been original to the factory. The national star on the fin looks to have been re-applied, this time with a thin white border, and a finely trimmed spinner was seen in addition. Many claims have been put forward that "22" belonged to HSU I. P. Motornii, but as of the time of writing the author is not convinced by these, and more research will be required on the matter to assign any reliable ownership of this handsome Yak-1B.

"Red 100" is the subject-- along with Yak-9 "64"-- of an extremely widely published set of still images extracted from some TASS 16 mm *cine* film shot just before the Battle of Kursk, 1943. For years it was thought that this machine might be a *razvedchik* (reconnaissance) model, but following a searching re-examination of the images, the author has determined that it was in fact a typical Yak-1B *massovii* aircraft. The camouflage scheme, which is extremely attractive, is likely a field applied job, and the rudder had been finished in red. The tactical number was rather crooked, and also in red colour, and the miniature star on the fin was trimmed in white.

"White 32" of Ivan D. Batychko of the 812 IAP, spring 1943. The aircraft wears an exceedingly strange field applied scheme of angular shapes and a 'wonky' star insignia, and one presumes therefore that it had been finished in MK-7 White originally at the factory. The regiment's classic 'reversed' 3 IAK badge was nicely applied to the nose, and the spinner finished in white. Batychko was sadly lost in aerial combat on 8 May 1943.

"White 12" was certainly photographed after the war-- apparently on display somewhere-- but nevertheless it retained its essential war-time appearance. A field applied NKAP style scheme is in view, along with typical national markings. Many Polish Yak-1Bs featured spinners with various trim, and most also the Polish 'checker-board' insignia.

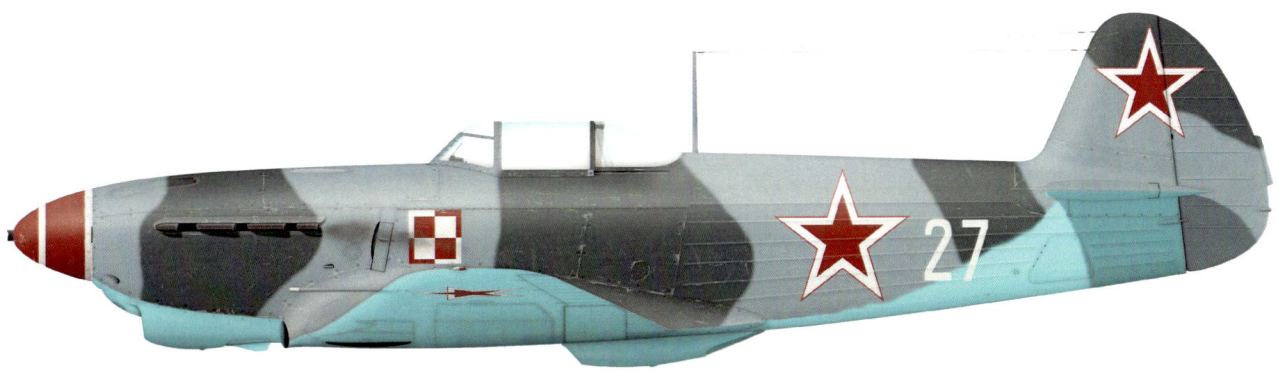

"White 27" was seen in Polish service just after the war, still wearing VVS style national stars. The appearance and colouration were absolutely classic for the time.

Another single-colour AMT-11 scheme, this fine example was photographed in Yugoslav service during 1946-47. The smartly applied national markings contribute to a very attractive appearance.

The Yak-1B, Normandie-Nemen Regiment Examples

The initial batch of Yak-1B fighters issued to the Normandie-Nemen regiment were early examples finished at the factory in MK-7 White winter schemes. "Red 17" was typical of these with its fairly worn surfaces, and was reportedly piloted by Yves Bizien. The inscription was a dedication to the defenders of Stalingrad from the collective farm workers of the *Krasnoyarskii* region.

"Red 44" was the personal Yak-1B of French ace Marcel Albert, early 1943. The finish, when photographed, must have been quite fresh and exhibited little wear. The French *tricolour* was seen on the fuselage port side, as well as the SPA.69 'pennant' emblem worn by Marcel's M.S. 406 aircraft in CG I/3. Marcel Albert was one of the few foreigners honoured with the title and award of Hero of the Soviet Union, and his final Official tally is still under intensive debate, appearing to number 7 + 16 Personal / Shared Claims (including three victories from service before Russia) in his VVS documentation.

Marcel Albert

Official Score: 7 + 16
Missions: ~200

Claims While Flying The Yak-1: 3 + 4

▲ ▼ Marcel Albert's subsequent Yak-1B was "White 6", which is known from a few indistinct images. In fact, it is not entirely clear if this was another aircraft, or a completely re-finished "Red 44" in temperate guise? Be that as it may, there is a known taxiing photograph of "6" from the port side without the later-- and famous-- "tiger" artwork. The nose decorations are seen in this well published image [right], which, for reasons unknown, is virtually always printed in mirror-reverse (it shows the *port* nose, not starboard). Another image is known from the port side showing the aircraft taking off and retracting its gear, and despite the poor quality of the photo this has been used to create the respective profile below. The entire scheme, with artwork, may be seen on the starboard side in a single (and rather poor) in-flight photo, and this is the basis of the profile above. All of these Yaks were received in winter white finish, and so subsequently were subjected to some rather dire (it must be said) field applied camouflage work. Moreover, all of the decorative painting appears to make use of the army lacquers to hand, so that the centre of the French *tricolour* was actually rendered in AMT-6 Black, for example. The dappling over the nose is well executed and provides for a nice effect, this in startling contrast to the horrendous camouflage scheme (especially to port). The dissimilar styles of the tactical numbers on either side of the fuselage are curious, and one wonders exactly how many times this machine must have been re-painted?

Over the years there has arisen much confusion about the identities of many Normandie-Niemen aircraft, especially the Yak-1B machines. 'Mouth' artwork is often seen in fragmentary bits, only, and problems distinguishing between different models of Yak fighters have beset many would-be profile artists. Following an extensive re-evaluation of the evidence, the author is certain that this odd machine was in fact Roland de La Poype's "White 24". The field applied scheme on this example was clearly quite ad-hoc, and frankly ugly, albeit improved slightly with its delightful nose artwork. Looking to the author for all the world like a *shark's* mouth, de La Poype in fact described his decoration as a *tigre volant*. A red-white-black *tricolour* and a fine white spinner tip complete this rather haphazard appearance.

Another temperate camouflaged Normandie-Niemen example was "White 29". The scheme application in this case was fairly neat, and not at all as absurd as some other examples. Interestingly, the *tricolour* again was completed with a black centre, emphasising the difficulty of obtaining custom paints at the local aerodrome.

"White 20" presents the sort of appearance that most would regard as prototypical for Normandie-Niemen Yak-1s, but in fact which the photographic record shows us to be quite exceptional. The field applied camouflage was common enough, but the use of the 303 IAD's bolt motif is very early, and suggests that this aircraft must have survived in the regiment until 1944. The broad white bordered star markings would also support that date. The *tricolour* remained black-centred, as applied, but the spinner shows a very light blue colour at the base, and the author believes this to have been applied with AMT-7.

The Yak-1, Captured Examples

This *massovii* Yak-1-- likely from Series 70, or thereabouts-- was widely photographed under evaluation by *Luftwaffe* personnel during 1942. The majority of the original camouflage finish was left intact, but the original VVS markings on the fuselage were obliterated with what appears to have been RLM 70 paint. German codes "EL+LI" were applied in white, and yellow tactical bands were added suitable for service on the Eastern Front.

"White 2" of the 3 IAK [see page 25] after its capture and re-painting by German forces during 1943. Considerable appliqué paint was seen over the upper surfaces, and in the profile above this has been depicted as RLM 70, which seems to fit the photographic tone best. The lower cowling was painted over with RLM 65. The Germans left the dedication text essentially intact for reasons unknown, but added their own theatre bands and national insignia.

The Yak-1 Family in Scale Line Drawings

The line drawings presented herein are entirely new, never before published. These represent the culmination of many years' labour, and are based virtually exclusively on direct measurements taken from various surviving examples, as well as from various parts and pieces held in private collections (such as Yak-1 **13-42**) and technical documentation. These drawings build on the fine and popular work published by *Modellist Konstruktur*, *Eksmo* and *AJ Press*, to name but a few.

Production of the I-26 began in Moscow's Factory № 301 (in Khimki, in fact, just north of the capitol) during 1940. The earliest models were built around the № 2 and № 3 prototypes, and indeed showed such immature features as seen in those machines. However, refinements and improvement commenced at once, the location of Yakovlev's experimental workshops in Moscow (the so-called "Factory № 115") being critical. And so it was that the I-26 transformed greatly during 1940, the last examples named "I-26" were rather different to the first, and bearing a considerable similarity to the "Yak-1" of the New Year (1941).

Simultaneously, production was launched at Factory № 292 in Saratov, home of the Yakovlev OKB. Additional examples were ordered from Factories № 30 in Moscow and № 47 at Chkalov, but no development took place at these facilities. During 1941 the programme was placed entirely in the hands of Yakovlev's bureau, and simultaneously renamed *Yak-1* to correspond to the new nomenclature system. By this time, of course, Saratov was already manufacturing examples which they referred to as *Massovii,* but these were by no means fully developed Yak-1s, and development and refinement continued with increasing urgency as war approached.

Total production of the Yak-1 was 8667 units through 192 Series. Manufacture of the type ended during 1944 at Saratov, supplanted at last by the aircraft's superb offspring, the Yak-3.

All of the primary scale line drawings in this volume are presented in 1:48 scale. In cases where scrap or detail views are rendered in another scale, these will be noted directly on the drawing.

As with all scale line drawings, it is often the case that certain details are deliberately omitted from oblique views where such items would be either difficult to render, or might be misleading in a flat projection. This is so, often, as a result of the curvature or shape of the structure, leading to problems of representing such detail in a two-dimensional plane. The small rivets present on under-wing panels or cowling seams when viewed from a side projection are examples of this kind of problem, and in these drawings have been omitted in those views. Similarly, radio aerials are omitted in top and front views, generally, as these take on the form of a bisecting panel line in such a projection and are often confusing. *Therefore, readers are advised to consult the most perpendicular line drawing available for the definitive level of detail over any given area of the aircraft.*

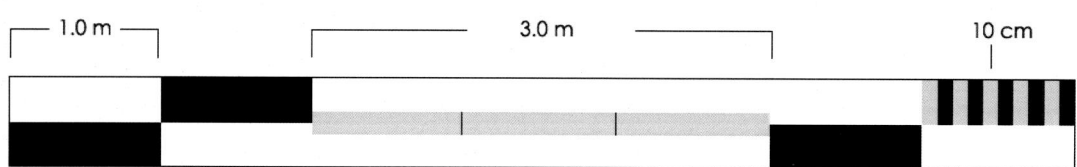

A Brief Examination of I-26 and Yak-1 Development

The period 1939 to 1941 was pivotal in the history of Soviet aircraft manufacture. This is a well documented truth, full of examples and descriptions. But, surely, the year 1940 itself must be viewed as *the* watershed year, encompassing so much of the confusion, reorganisation and technological innovation which marked this epoch in Russian aviation. And it is for this reason, undoubtedly, that the I-26 programme spun itself into such remarkable disorder and variation, as the primary development of this high performance prototype seemed to have been compressed mainly into this very calendar year.

Chaos, however, is often one face of a coin whose flip side is creative genius. The I-26 programme demonstrates both of these attributes with aplomb, and indeed so in a wider sense, encompassing not only the industry's struggles and organisational development, but also the government's, and its own ideas about how it should oversee and operate the business of aviation design. When the first I-26 prototype appeared in January 1940, the government was still convinced by the *design-by-committee* method so common in such gigantic bureaucracies. However, by the end of the same year, most aircraft development was left to the specific design bureaux of each respective aircraft project-- such as Lavochkin's or Yakolev's-- and a technical representative of the government served *in situ* with these OKBs and their factories.

It is in precisely this way that one **A.T. Stepanets**, Senior Engineer, came to be associated with the Yak fighter programme. And it is, of course, from his own seminal work on the topic-- *Istrabiteli Yak Perioda VoV*-- that we now know and understand the complex history of the I-26 / Yak-1 family. To this we must add the extremely fine efforts of historians **Sergei Kuznetsov** and **Ivan Rodinov**, whose work [see *Recommended Reading*] on the Yak-1 (and related production) has been outstanding, and informative. Taking these together, it is now possible to identify and understand the various developmental stages and versions of this aircraft.

Following an evaluation of the I-26 № 2 prototype, the NKAP decided to undertake series manufacture of this fighter. An initial plan was drawn up to launch I-26 production at Factory № 301, near Moscow. This was an experienced facility with many renowned engineers, and currently involved in starting production also of the I-301 (LaGG-3). The № 2 and № 3 prototypes were investigated thoroughly by the factory staff, and in the process of doing so the government issued instructions for three initial series of fighters.

Series 1, of 12 units, was to consist of I-26 machines based upon the two prototypes (No 2 and No 3). Modifications were to be kept to an absolute minimum, the main idea being to assemble the necessary jigs, tooling and other industrial items needed for mass manufacture of the type. Factory № 301 referred to this Series as the "Small", or "Short-run" (*malaya seriya)* batch, this indicating their embryonic nature. The next batch, Series two and three, each of 18 units, was to form the basis of large-scale manufacture. The NKAP indicated that line techniques and other related assembly problems should be properly sorted during this phase, which the factory referred to as the "Base" (*nulevaya seriya*) series. The third batch was to consist of Series five to seven (prior to this a 4th Series was actually built), of 25 units each, and these aircraft were meant to be fully combat ready machines intended for introduction into the Army Air Force (VVS). Factory № 301 knew these aircraft as the "Service" (*voiskovaya seriya*) series.

Almost simultaneously, the government decided to launch manufacture of the I-26 fighter at Yakovlev's Factory № 292 in Saratov. As the work of his own bureau, this order seems logical enough, and the fact of sharing out production between Saratov and Moscow in this way should be understood really as the keen desire on the part of the VVS to introduce modern equipment at the soonest moment given the dire political situation in Europe. Or, in other words, this was something of a *production-by-committee* effort, in keeping with government policies of the time.

The first two series (only 5 examples each) built at Factory № 292 are a mystery. To date, the author has found no information-- neither photographic nor documentary-- to explain these machines and their relative details. Such abbreviated production certainly suggests that they were developmental, likely with an eye to getting the various tooling, jigs and other manufacturing items ready for series production. But, they are curious for another reason, as well: Saratov I-26s of Series 3 demonstrated a major aerodynamic modification to the stabiliser and elevators. This new unit came into existence at the very same time on the UTI-26-2 prototype, just as Sr. Eng. Stepanets joined the Yakovlev OKB programme in Moscow on behalf of the NII VVS. Ergo, we are left to ask if the new stabilisers were a developmental idea by Saratov, by Stepanets *et al* in the Moscow workshop, or if they hail from another source? At the moment, we do not know (albeit the author suspects these resulted from Stepanets' and Sinel'shikov's work on the new UTI prototype). Be that as it may, and minus any early embryonic examples, Factory № 292 did not produce any I-26 fighters with the old style prototype stabilisers. There were still fluid design changes to the oil coolers and radiators, as at Factory № 301, but by Series 8 the facility was turning out aircraft which anyone would recognise as typical *Yak-1* pattern fighters.

From January 1941 things in the I-26 programme changed radically again. During 1940, Factory № 47 was tasked by the government to build I-26s according to plans and instructions sent via Factory № 301. In the event, this facility managed to complete only two examples. Likewise, Factory № 30 in Moscow was directed to build I-26s according to instructions passed from the Yakovlev OKB at Saratov. These machines are thought to be roughly similar to Series 5-7 examples from factory № 292, and the plant completed some 65 such aircraft by the beginning of 1941. With the New Year the government decided to terminate I-26 production in Moscow altogether (and at Chkalov) and placed the entire programme into the hands of Factory № 292 at Saratov (where the OKB was of course located). And finally, the aircraft was now to be known by its new nomenclature made up of the designer's initials, and thus the *I-26* henceforth became the *Yak-1*.

Despite the logical centralisation on manufacture and development in Saratov, some curiosities in production examples remained. Of these, the fitment-- or not-- of bomb rack equipment is a vexation. The NKAP issued instructions to Factory № 292 that from Series 5 all aircraft were to be built with an internal wing fitting that could accommodate a BI-42 bomb mount, this to enable a bomb of up to 100 kg weight (ergo a FAB-100). However, the remaining evidence casts very considerable doubt as to whether this instruction was actually carried out. Stepanets cautions suitably that such bomb equipment was *rarely* employed (due to performance reductions), but the truth might have been even less frequent than that. In the first case, the author has physically examined the related wing pieces on 13-42, 11-13, 15-18, 39-78 and even Yak-1B 22-106, and *none* of these examples were so outfitted. German wartime documentation on

[Left] A Yak-7A (likely p/n 14-11) under investigation at the LII, 1942. The BI-42 bomb racks are evident here showing their position and details.
[Right] A typical Yak-1 wing (this example from Series 50 onwards) with no external sign of such mounting hardware, as usual.

Of all the German technical material seen by the author regarding the Yak-1, this image alone *might* show such fittings on the wing's lower surface. Are these threaded holes in a solid block between ribs? Has the wing been segmented in this way for this reason? Alas, at the time of writing we simply do not know.

the Yak-1 wing does not mention nor show such fittings, and neither does their considerable photographic coverage of such parts. Photographs exist taken at the Saratov factory from 1942 right through 1944, and none of these images show such fittings in place. Installation of these internal fittings was specifically suspended during the manufacture of the *massovii Oblegchenyi* examples (Series 126-147), but Stepanets tells us that it was reinstated thereafter. A considerable mystery. Moreover, one cannot see such fittings on a finished Yak-1 unless the BI-42 mount had been installed, as the internal parts were hidden by the wing's fabric covering and only pierced when needed (as on the Lavochkin's wing). Except under investigation (at the NII VVS, LII or NIPAV, etc), the author is aware of no wartime photograph showing Yak-1s with the BI-42 mount in place.

With Series 20 a host new detail modifications were realised, and externally these examples can be identified by a new spinner with a long Hucks collar. The internal changes were many, and despite the fact that Factory No 292 referred to examples from Series 12 onwards as *massovii* versions, in retrospect we can really state that this description should be applied to Series 20 aircraft (and thereafter) with all of these refinements.

Most I-26s and many early Yak-1s lacked a radio, and this matter concerned the NKAP greatly. There were many reasons for this omission, often devolving around the patchy functionality of the early RSI-4 radio sets. However, the government wanted radio sets installed, as in fact the relevant Production Contracts specified, and issued orders to Saratov that from September 1940 one-in-five I-26 examples was to have an RSI-4 fitted. From October the number of radio equipped fighters was to be 1:3, and indeed from December all production examples should be so fitted. The photographic record, of course, shows us that these goals were not met, and this situation is confirmed by the very large number of complaints emanating from the government on this topic. In fact, RSI-4 sets did not actually become commonplace (let alone *standard*) until about Series 60, or so, and even thereafter examples can be seen without radios and their associated hardware installed.

From Series 43 the government decided that all Yak-1s should be fitted with RS rocket armament. Six RO82 rails were therefore mounted under the outer wings. Many regiments in practice removed these rails as they incurred very significant drag, but production units had these fitted despite that fact until they were discontinued with Series 65.

Series 49 introduced a major modification in the shape of new half-round aft canopy windows replacing the earlier clear section. At the same time a large radio mast was developed, these being increasingly common on subsequent models as more and more radios were fitted.

The onset of winter during 1941 brought with it the introduction of 'winterised' Yak-1 versions with ski landing gear. Some experimental versions had been built as early as September, these machines still wearing temperate camouflage and featuring earlier version details. The main series of winter versions-- the *massovii* 'winterised'-- began with Series 55 in November; aircraft No 38-55 being widely photographed at the NII VVS. Production of winterised Yak-1s continued until Series 71 at the end of February 1942. It should be noted that ski gear kits were also issued by the factory, and regiments in the field could fit these units to existing machines, resulting in some odd detail combinations. Winterised versions built up to Series 65 were fitted with RS rockets, additionally.

With the termination of winter production the Yak-1 reverted to what was essentially a Series 49 standard, but minus RS rocket armament. The next major change in production occurred with Series 85 (August 1942) when the M-105PF engine was fitted as standard. Series 90 introduced a new rudder navigation lamp, and also an opening on the starboard forward fuselage for that side's ShKAS machine gun ammunition tank (which hitherto was accessed from port).

Series 96 was a rather special batch of Yak-1s. These aircraft were built with a mind to reduce the weight of the fighter to the maximum degree possible, thus producing an *oblegchennyi* (lightened) version. A small test batch of 10 such aircraft were built in March 1942, but Series 96 meant to realise these weight economies to the full. Any item deemed to be extraneous to performance was removed, including the radio, the ShKAS machine guns, their related systems and other small details. These examples were specifically not finished with bomb mounting fixtures. To save additional weight the all-metal fin and stabiliser from a Yak-7 were fitted, although a few of these aircraft did not receive such units and retained wooden items.

Aerodynamic testing and improvement had been an on-going affair, and with Series 99 a major change in the aircraft's appearance was introduced. The New Yak-1B model [in fact, the 'B' suffix related to the fitment of the new armament, ironically] introduced a cut-down rear fuselage with a new clear aft glazing. Armour-glass was installed both ahead of the pilot in the windscreen and behind the pilot's head (as the armoured seat back was accordingly reduced in height). The two ShKAS guns were discarded and replaced by a single 12.7 mm UBS gun to port. At the same time various drag reducing refinements had been tested, particularly on example No 08-68 [see Appendix II], and these modifications of the *ulyushennoy aehrodinamikoi* (UA, or improved aerodynamics) line of research were ordered by the government to be applied to the new model at the earliest moment. Some partial and mixed-detail units were thus completed, but by Series 111 all of the new -1B models featured the full compliment of modifications. In this form, production of the Yak-1B continued-- with an increase in ammunition storage at Series 127-- until terminated in 1944.

During 1943-44 some 385 Yak-1 MPVO versions were completed, these usually being modified on the production lines during final assembly. The MPVO was intended for service with Army PVO forces and these were equipped for night and poor weather operations with the RPK-10 compass, FS-155 radio, AG-5 artificial horizon, VR-2 variometer and other related instruments. These models were externally indistinguishable from the usual contemporary versions.

One last batch of *oblegchennyi* aircraft completed the programme, these the *massovii obl.* examples of Series 127 to 147 (March to July 1943). During this period Saratov was ordered to built lightened models alongside normal versions, these to the tune of 5 examples per day, and from July 10 examples per day. Given the timing, one may see that these machines were not only lightened, but also possessed the aerodynamic refinements of UA manufacture, and these models were highly prized by Soviet pilots.

A final word on I-26 and Yak-1 manufacture: readers should consider the Production Numbers (or Factory Numbers) seen throughout this work with care. Moscow built (No 301) aircraft were identified by the formula **Series**, **Example** (e.g. "0209" was I-26 number 9 of Series 2), while Saratov built aircraft were given as **Example - Series** (usually with a dash, e.g. "02-09" was number 2 of Series 9).

I-26 Prototypes, Factory № 115 (Moscow)

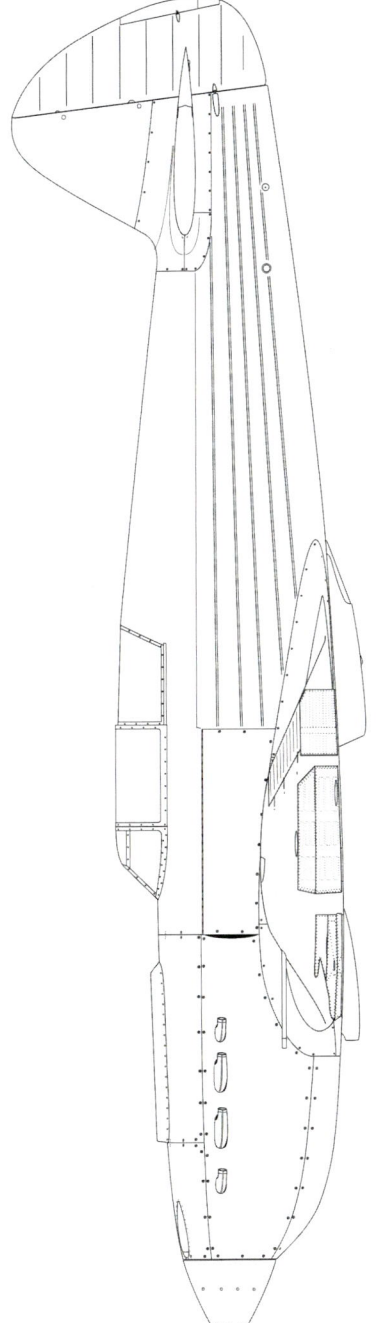

The I-26 No 1 prototype as flown on 13 January 1940 . The orignal vertical stabiliser looks most un-Yak-like to modern eyes.

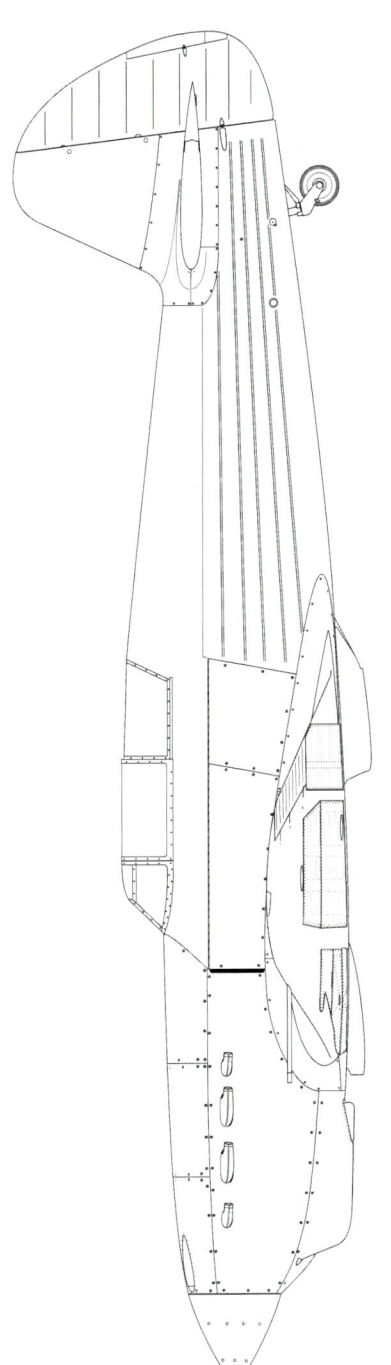

The I-26 No 2 rebuilt prototype, ca. June 1940. The revised fin unit introduced the classic Yakolev shape which we know today, and a hallmark of the entire family since then.

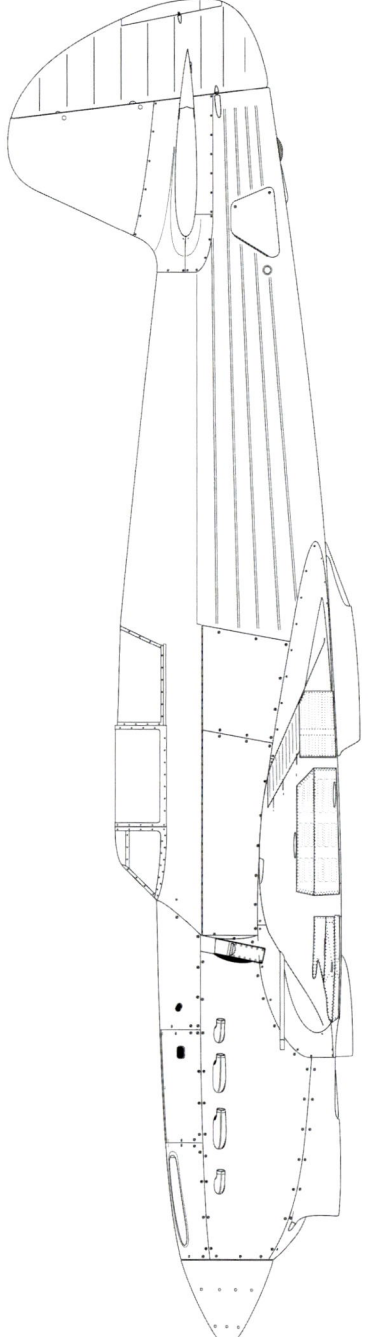

The I-26 No 3 prototype looked very much more like a production aircraft by August 1940. The service version's armament package was perfected on this aircraft-- including the small upper cowling openings for the link ejection slot and gas port exit-- as well as the engine mounting hardware, propeller and other sundry details. The wings still possessed inadequately thin skinning, a defect which was inadvertently copied in early Moscow I-26 manufacture.

Engine:
- *Klimov M-105P, 1050 hp for take-off & emergency*

Armament:
- *2 x 7.62 mm ShKAS machine-guns (synchronised) with 750 rds per gun*
- *1 x 20 mm ShVAK cannon firing through spinner with 110 rounds*

I-26 No 3 Upper View

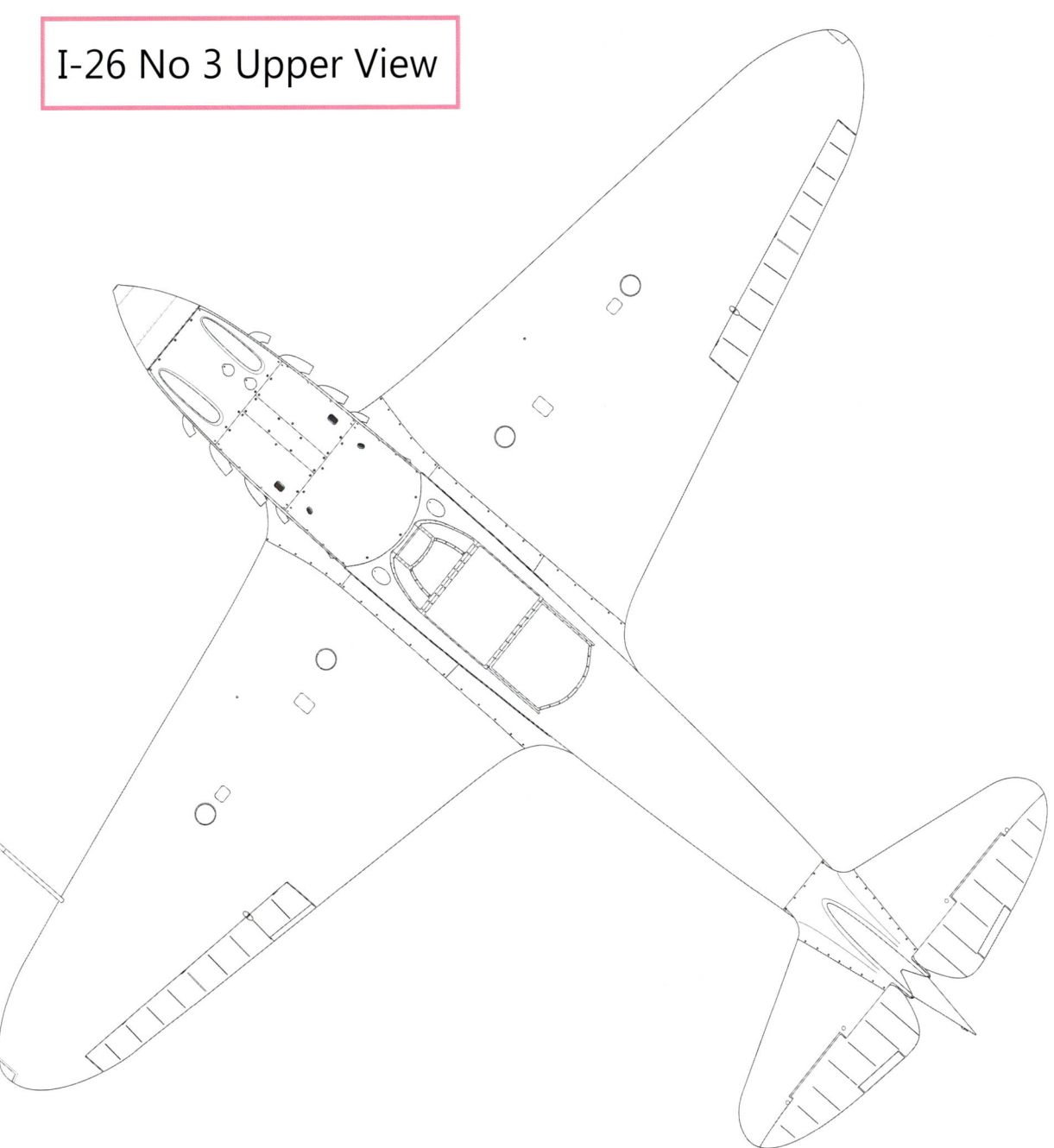

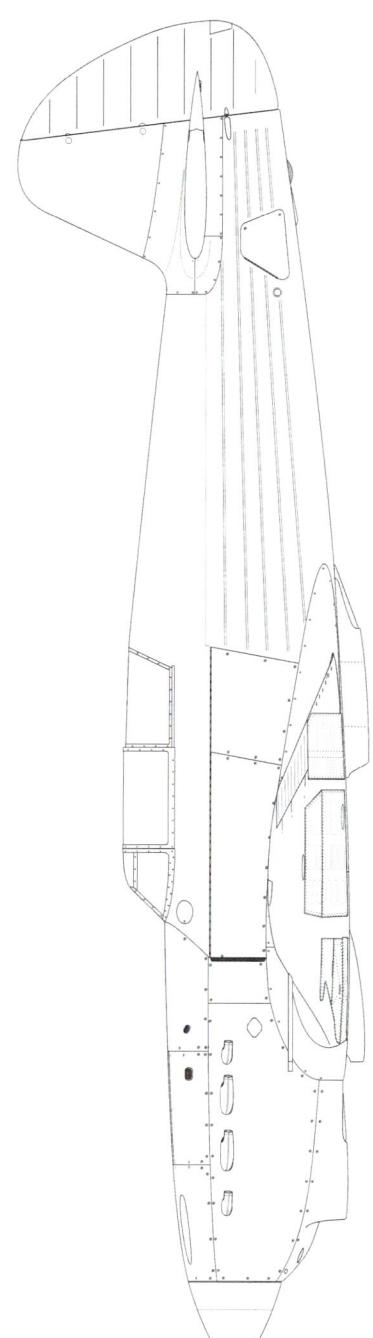

Malaya Seriya

Factory No 301's initial batch of 12 examples. The small oil cooler under the nose is evident, as is the reduced radiator bath. An intake for the engine and accessories was placed aft of the oil cooler, as seen on the initial I-26-2 prototype. The tail wheel was of a mostly retracting type, with the tyre just exposed without full doors. Small gun barrel troughs and a large port side ammunition bay cover were typical of early Moscow production.

Engine:
- *Klimov M-105P, 1050 hp for take-off & emergency*

Armament:
- *2 x 7.62 mm ShKAS machine-guns (synchronised) with 750 rds per gun*
- *1 x 20 mm ShVAK cannon firing through spinner with 110 rounds*

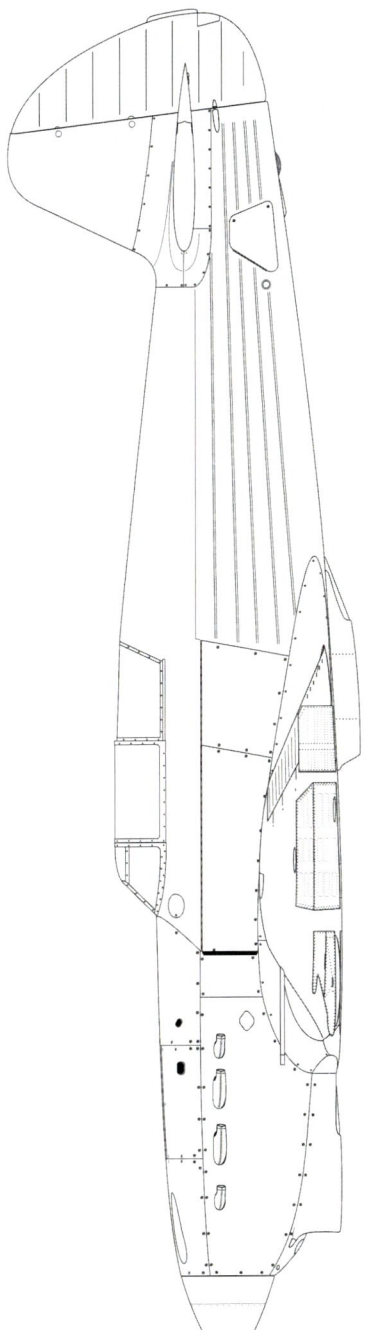

Nulevaya Seriya

Series 2 to 4 were similar to the first, but dispensed with the awkward engine intake scoop under the nose for one now placed into the port wing root. This intake would vary in size and shape throughout early I-26 manufacture. Inner gear bay door covering the main gear tyres were still seen on these examples.

Engine:
- *Klimov M-105P, 1050 hp for take-off & emergency*

Armament:
- *2 x 7.62 mm ShKAS machine-guns (synchronised) with 750 rds per gun*
- *1 x 20 mm ShVAK cannon firing through spinner with 110 rounds*

Main Features:

- *Small gun port openings*
- *Square ammunition tray cover (port)*
- *Aerodynamic conical ('Moscow style') spinner without Hucks collar*
- *Aileron trim tab, port only*
- *I-26 prototype style stabilisers*
- *Main gear inner doors over tyres*
- *Mostly retracted tail wheel*
- *Reduced radiator size*
- *Ground adjustable rudder trim tab*

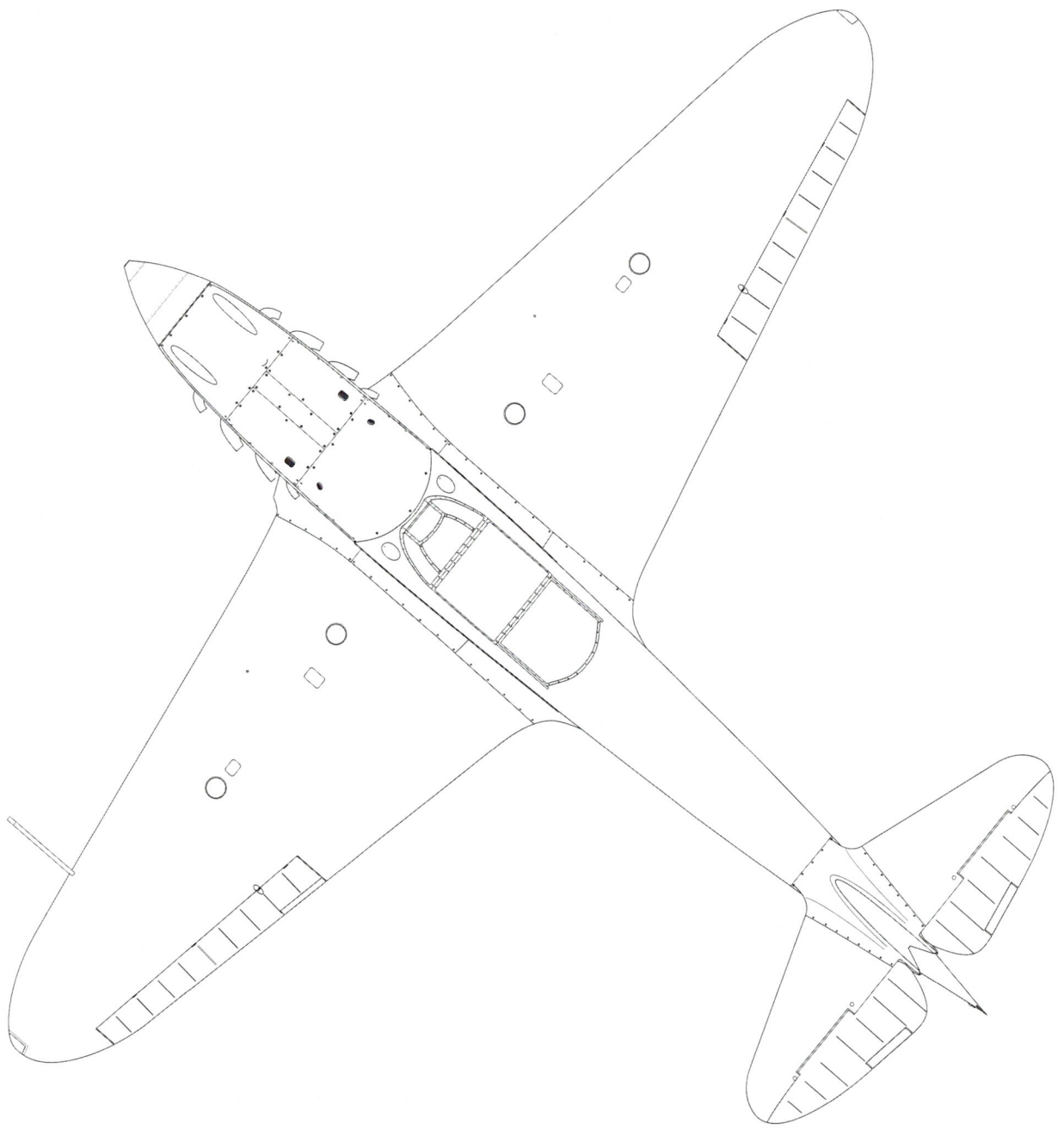

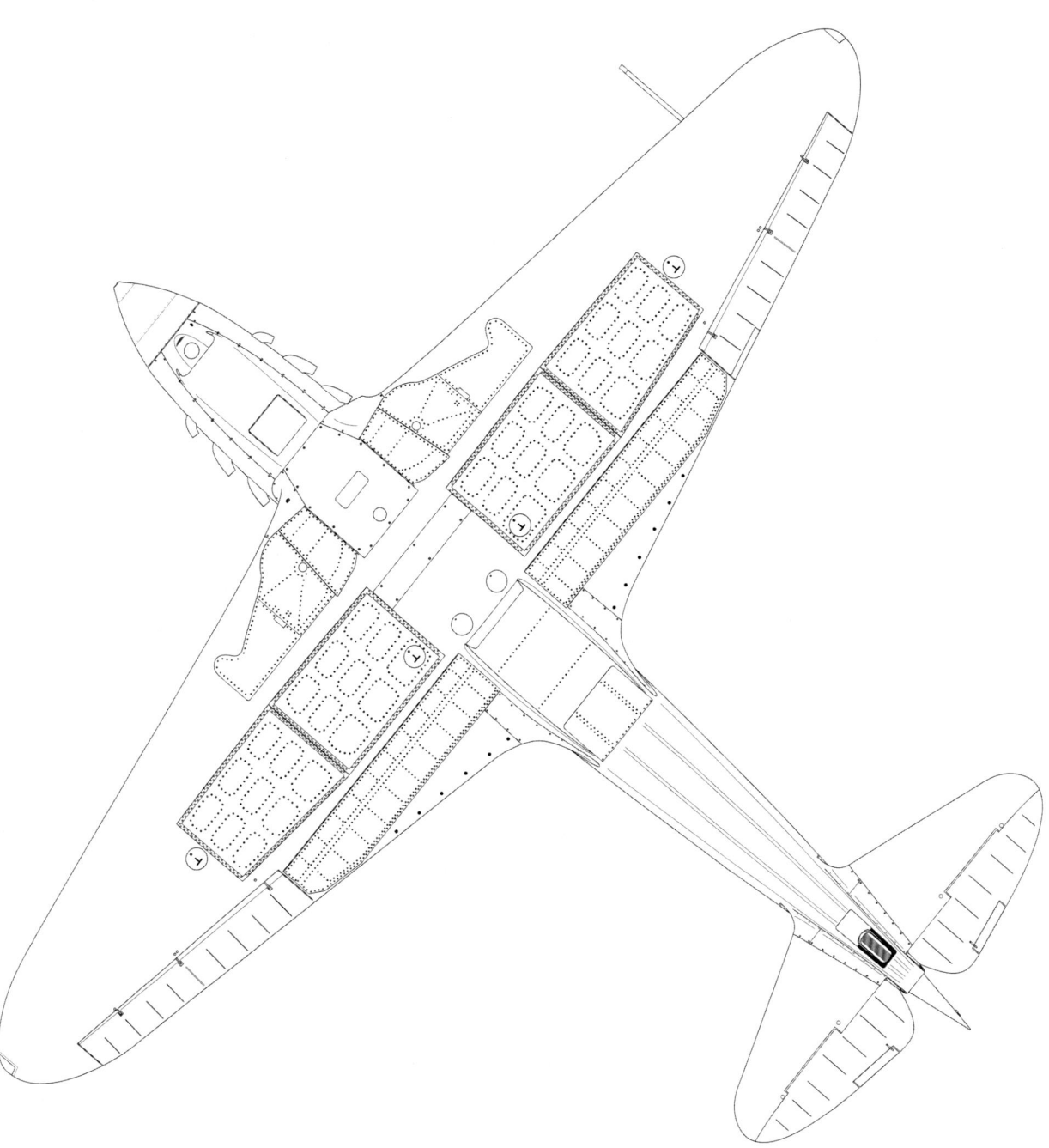

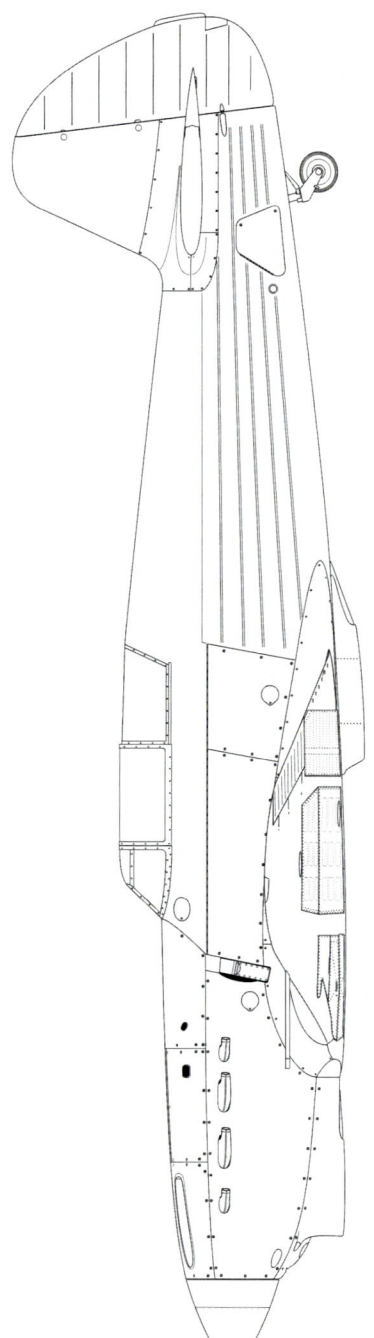

Voiskovaya Seriya

Series 5 to 7 were meant to be service ready production examples, and indeed these were distributed to active VVS regiments (notably the 11 IAP around Moscow). In the event, these models (certainly from Series 5 and 6, as depicted in these drawings) were still immature and not entirely satisfactory, but many did see action. New and larger gun openings were evident, along with a fixed tail wheel.

Engine:
- *Klimov M-105P, 1050 hp for take-off & emergency*

Armament:
- *2 x 7.62 mm ShKAS machine-guns (synchronised) with 750 rds per gun*
- *1 x 20 mm ShVAK cannon firing through spinner with 110 rounds*

Main Feature Changes:

- *Larger gun port openings*
- *Smaller ammunition opening with port tray exposed (port side only)*
- *Two small covers on upper cowling*
- *Main gear inner door covers deleted*
- *Fixed tail wheel*
- *New round panel access covers to port*
- *New accessories intake on lower port nose*

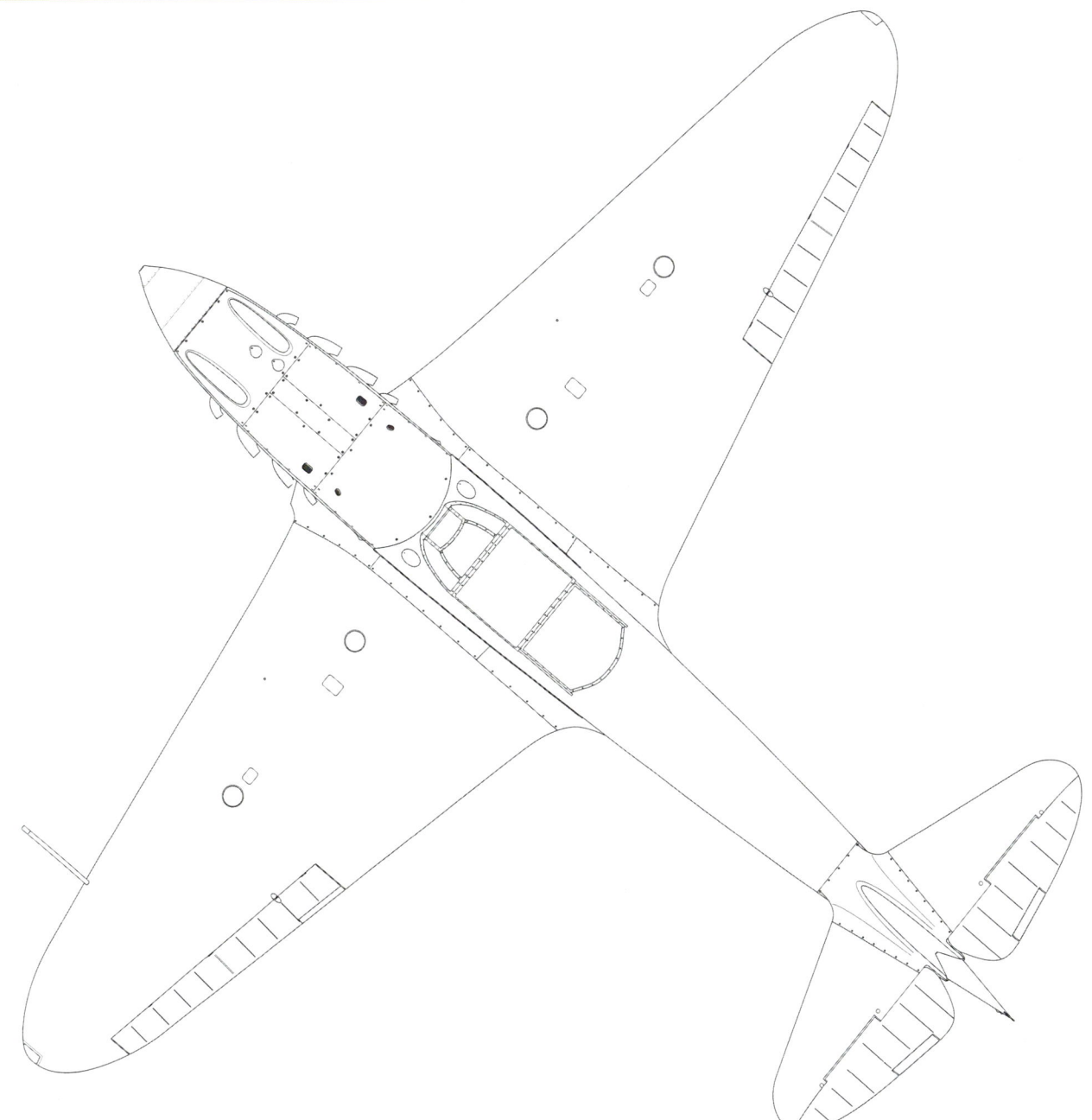

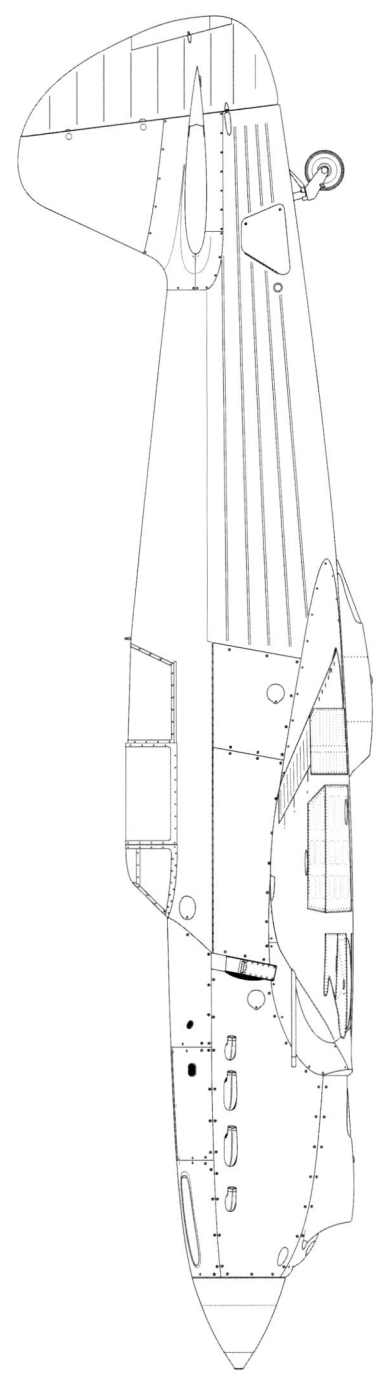

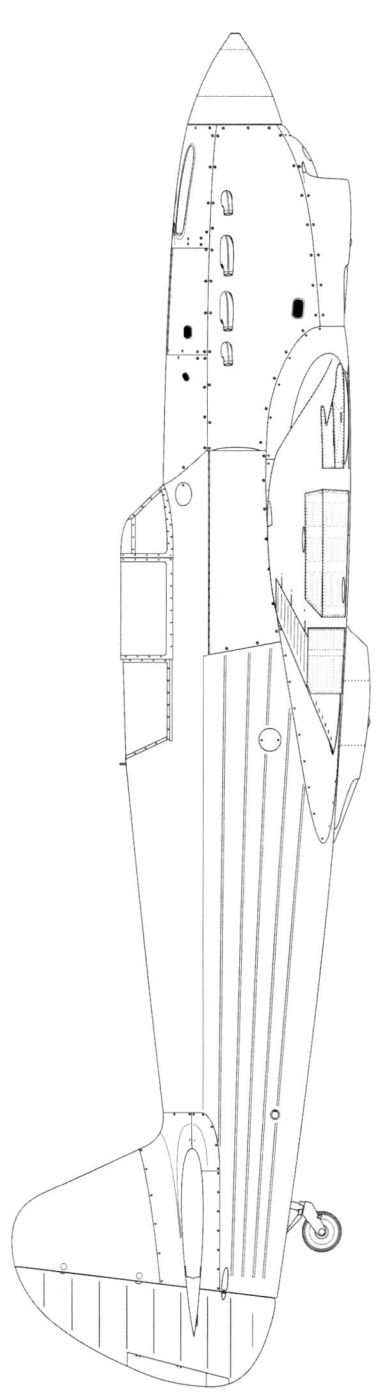

Main Feature Changes:
- *Flight adjustable rudder trim tab*
- *Round access cover to starboard below aft cockpit*
- *Revised port wing root intake*
- *Removed inner gear doors over tyres*
- *Reshaped oil cooler*
- *Larger 'Saratov' style radiator*
- *Many examples from Series 7 featured a small stub dipole radio mast attachment*

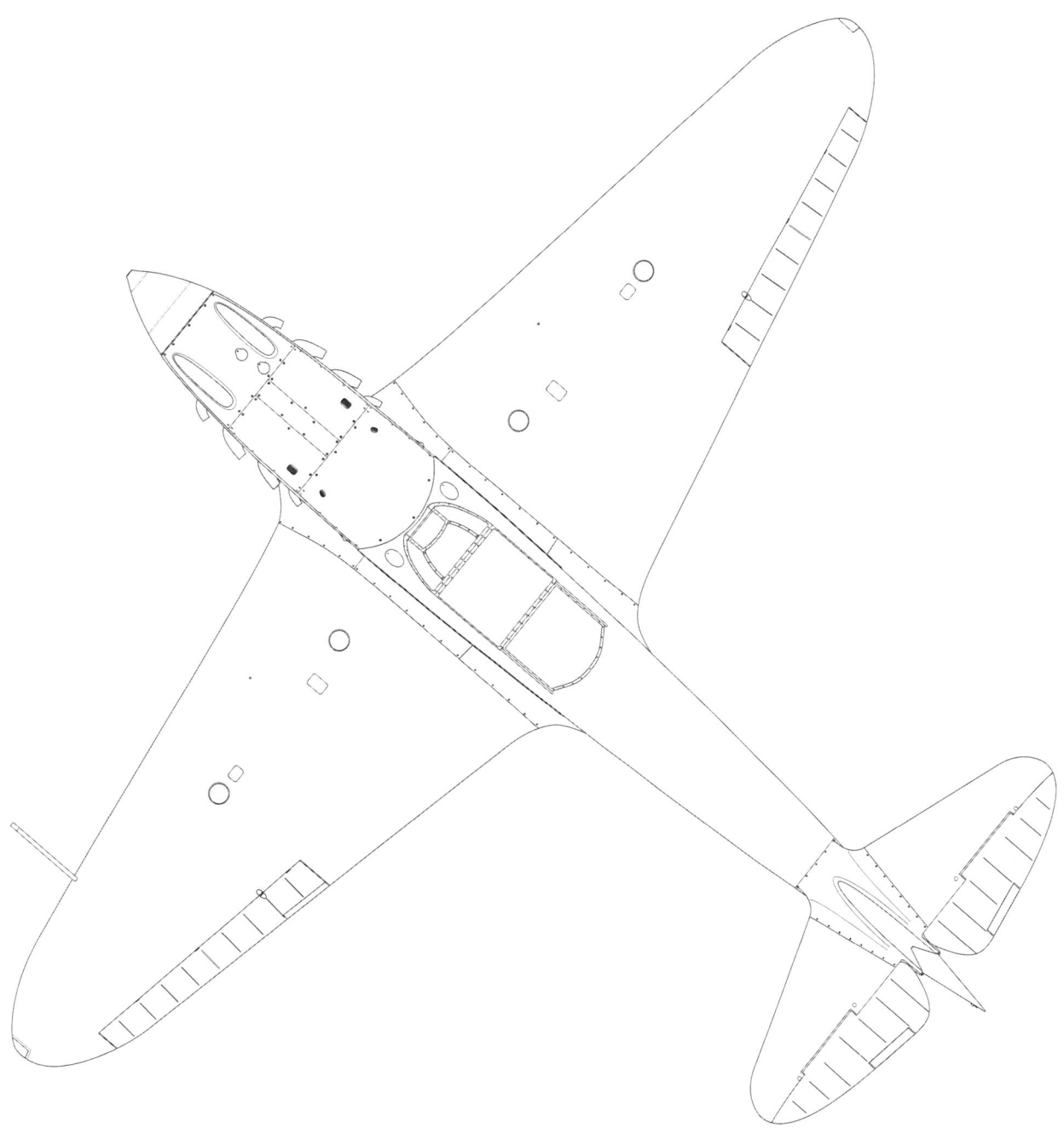

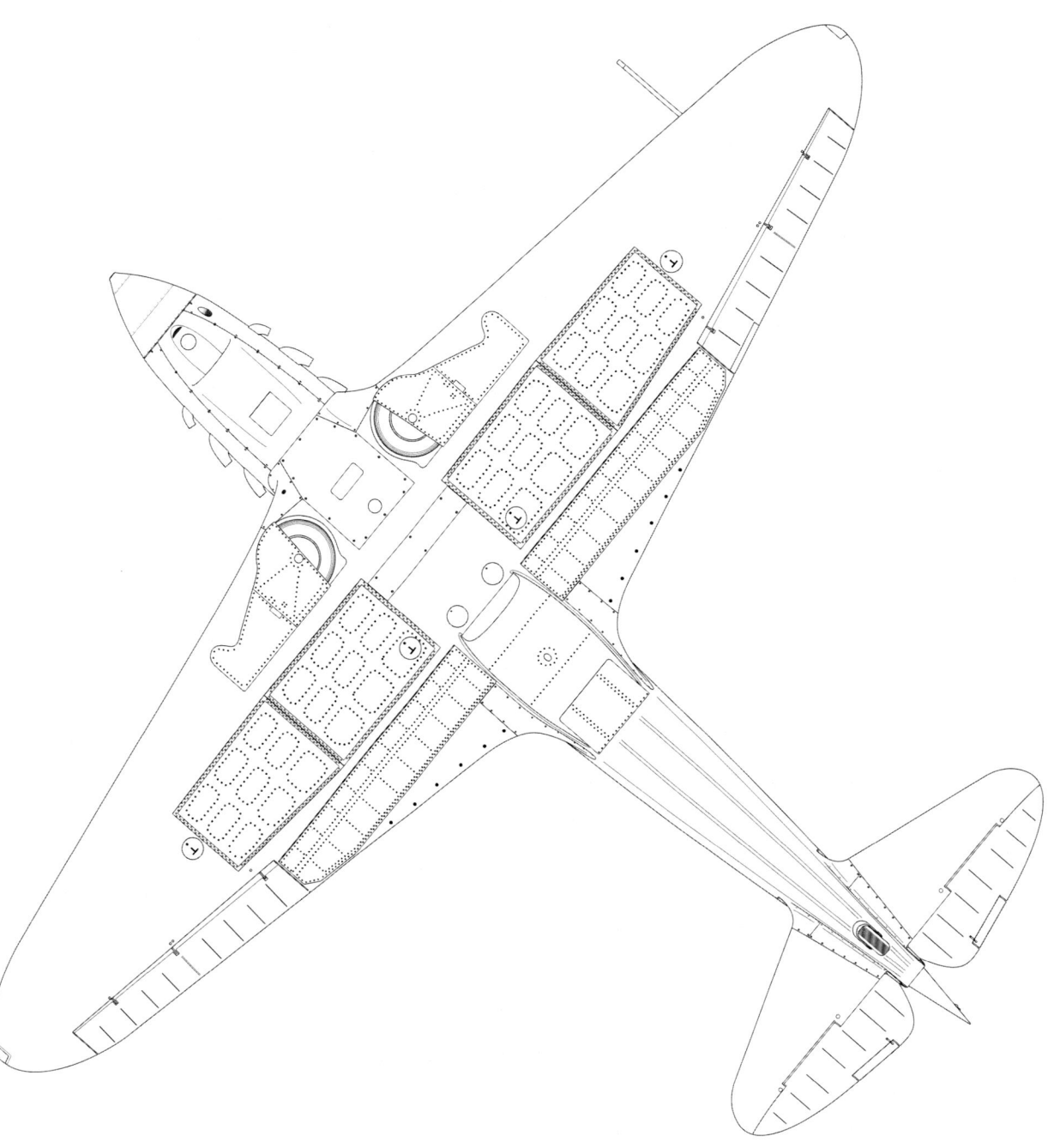

Voiskovaya Seriya *(continued)*

- *Klimov M-105P, 1050 hp for take-off & emergency*

Armament:
- *2 x 7.62 mm ShKAS machine-guns (synchronised) with 750 rds per gun*
- *1 x 20 mm ShVAK cannon firing through spinner with 110 rounds*

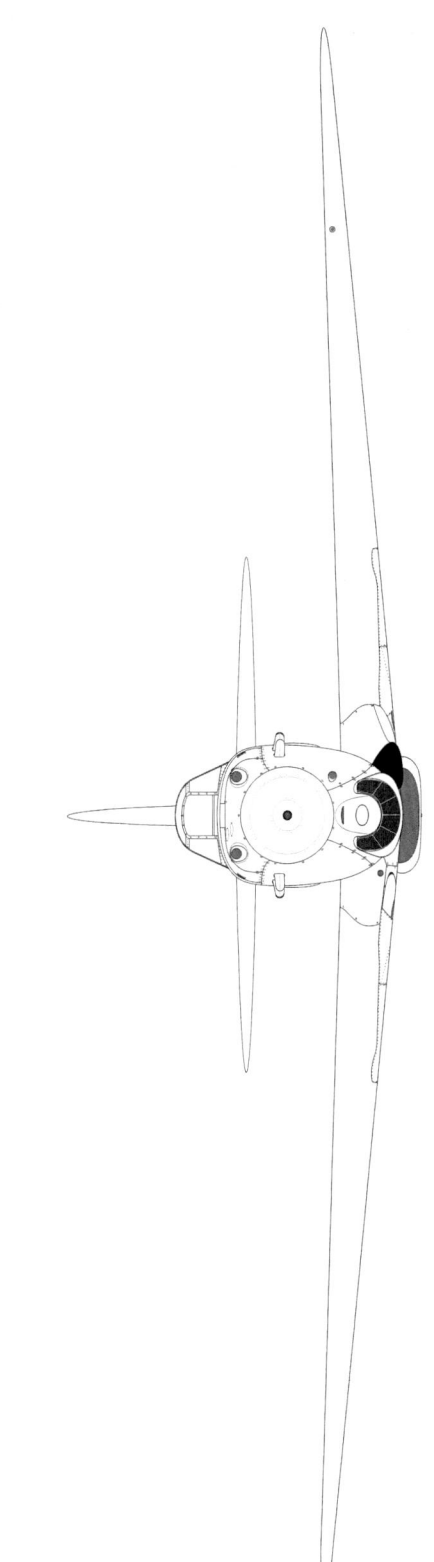

I-26 Saratov Production Series 3, Factory № 292

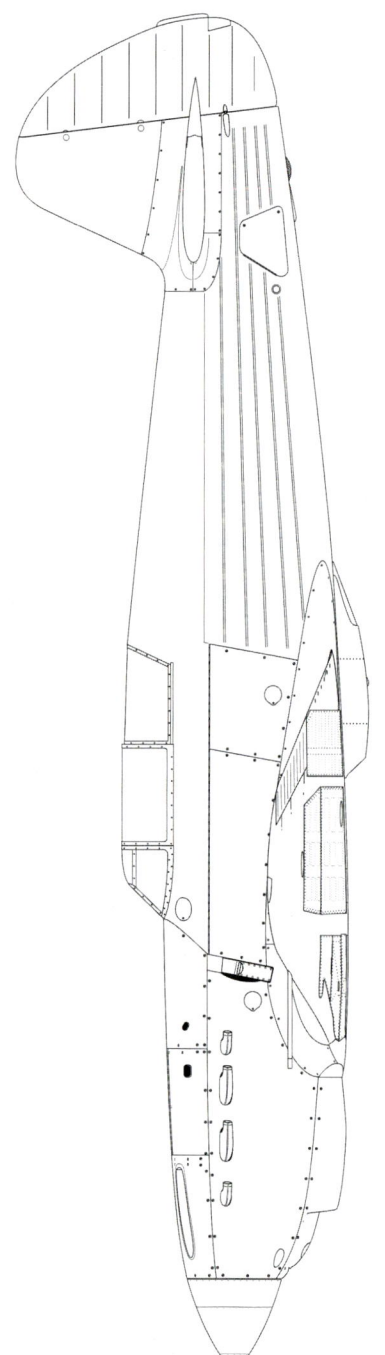

Series 3 examples built in Saratov were similar in most respects to early Factory No 301 machines, but critically different in regards to the revised stabiliser. The oil cooler was of a smaller pattern, but not the radiator, which was already of increased size and shape. The armament details were up-to-date, but these aircraft retained a fixed rudder trim tab and mostly retractable tail wheel.

Engine:
- *Klimov M-105P, 1050 hp for take-off & emergency*

Armament:
- *2 x 7.62 mm ShKAS machine-guns (synchronised) with 750 rds per gun*
- *1 x 20 mm ShVAK cannon firing through spinner with 110 rounds*

Main Features:
- *Revised 'Saratov' type stabilisers*
- *Main gear inner doors over tyres*
- *Mostly retracted tail wheel*
- *Small oil cooler*
- *Ground adjustable rudder trim tab*
- *Revised port wing root intake*

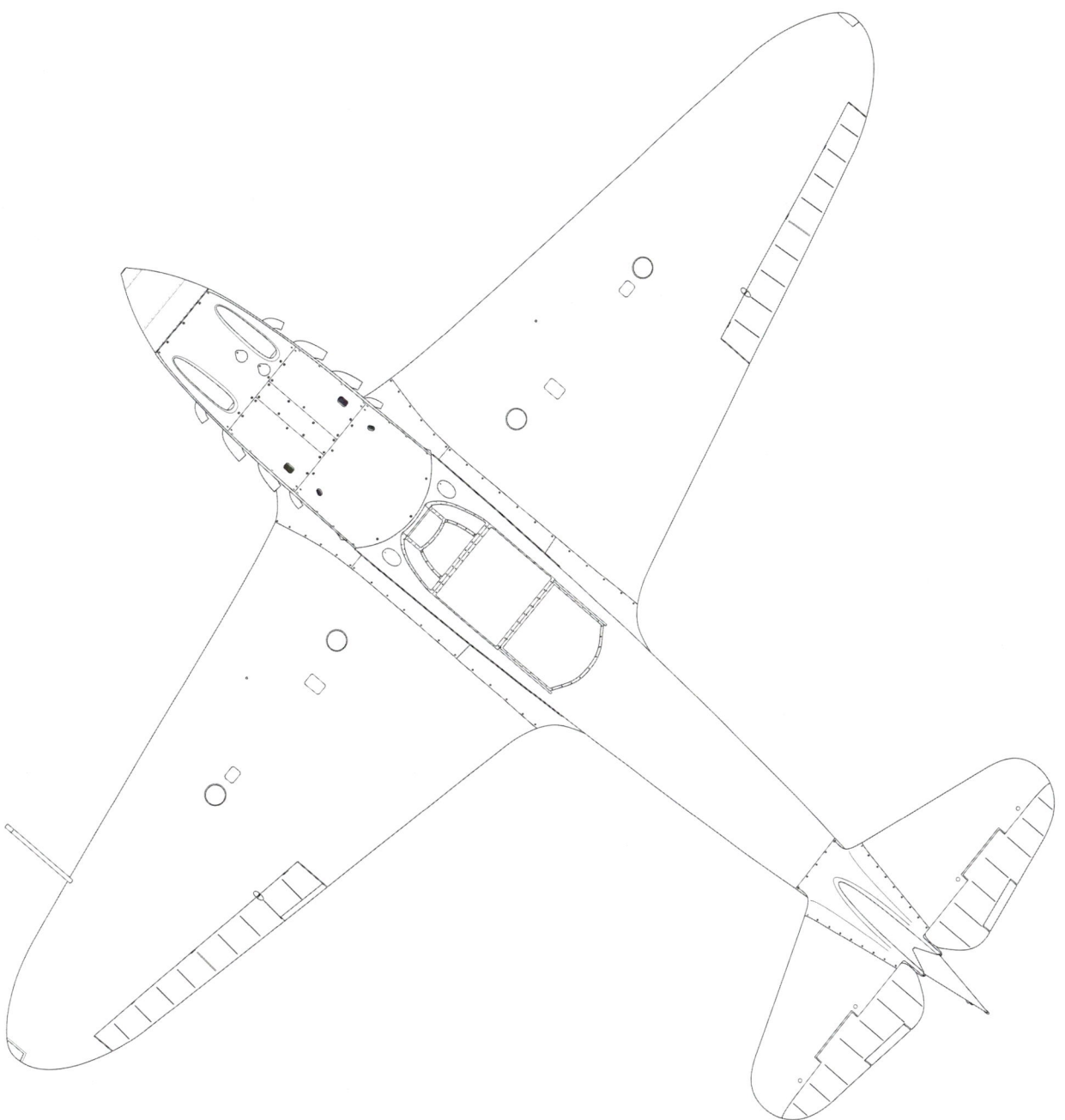

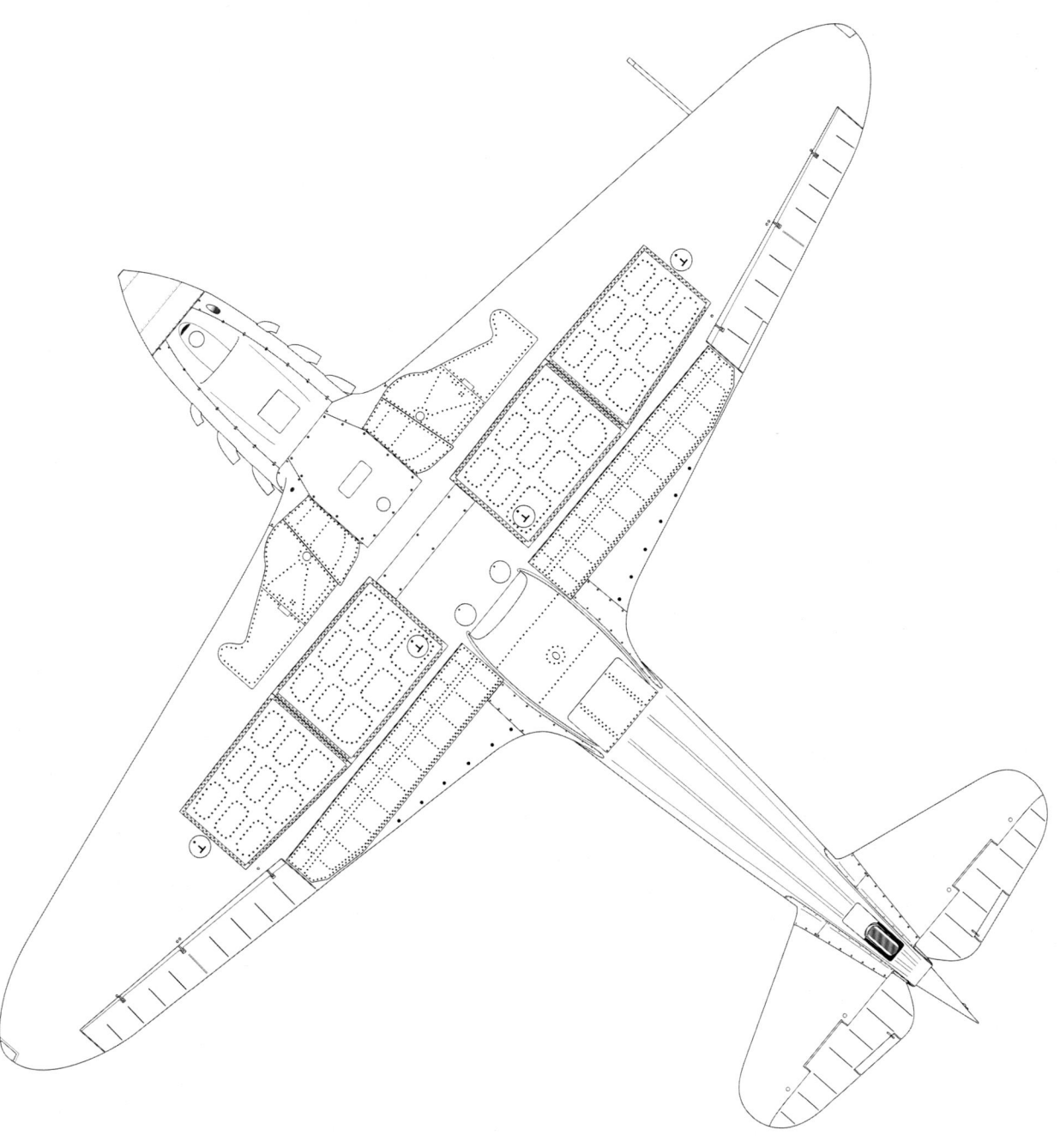

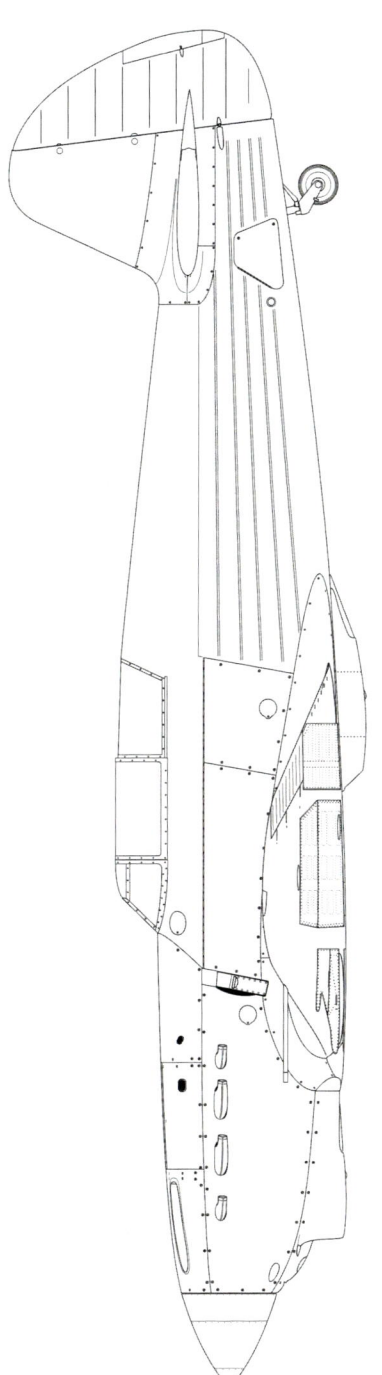

Despite still being called the "I-26", Factory No 292's Series 8 machines were essentially identical in detail to the first Yak-1 models [see next]. A fixed tail wheel replaced the retracting unit and the inner main gear cover doors were omitted. A flight adjustable rudder trim tab was installed.

Yak-1 Series 9, Factory № 292

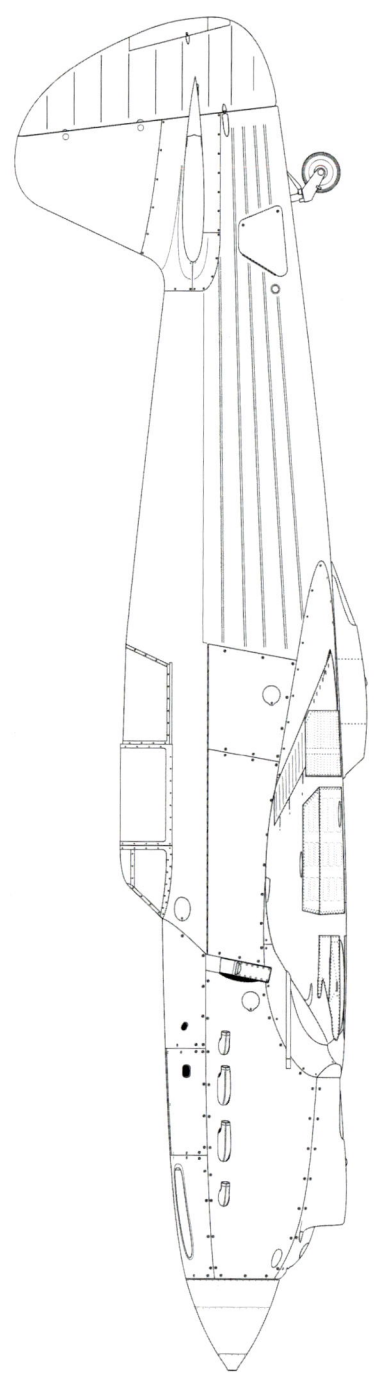

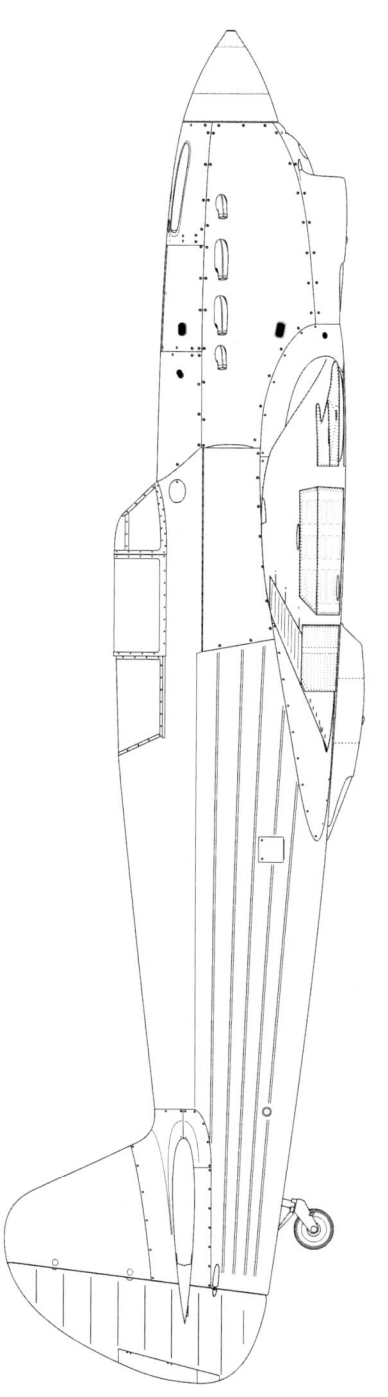

Main Feature Changes:
- *Flight adjustable rudder trim tab*
- *Fixed tail wheel*
- *Revised port wing root intake*
- *Reshaped oil cooler*
- *Port wing leading edge landing light (typical from Series 9, standard from Series 12)*
- *Main gear inner doors omitted*
- *Square access hatch to starboard*

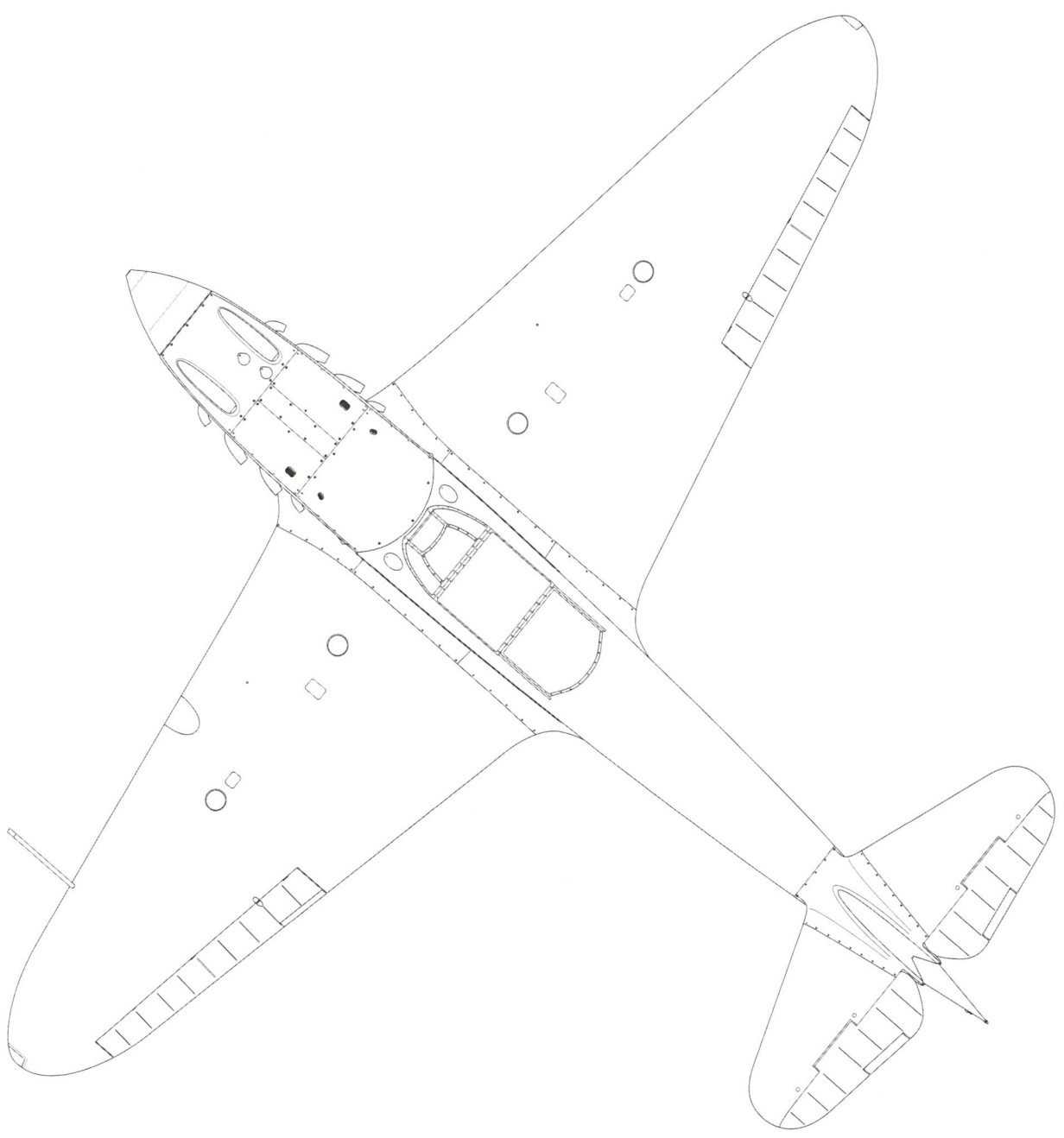

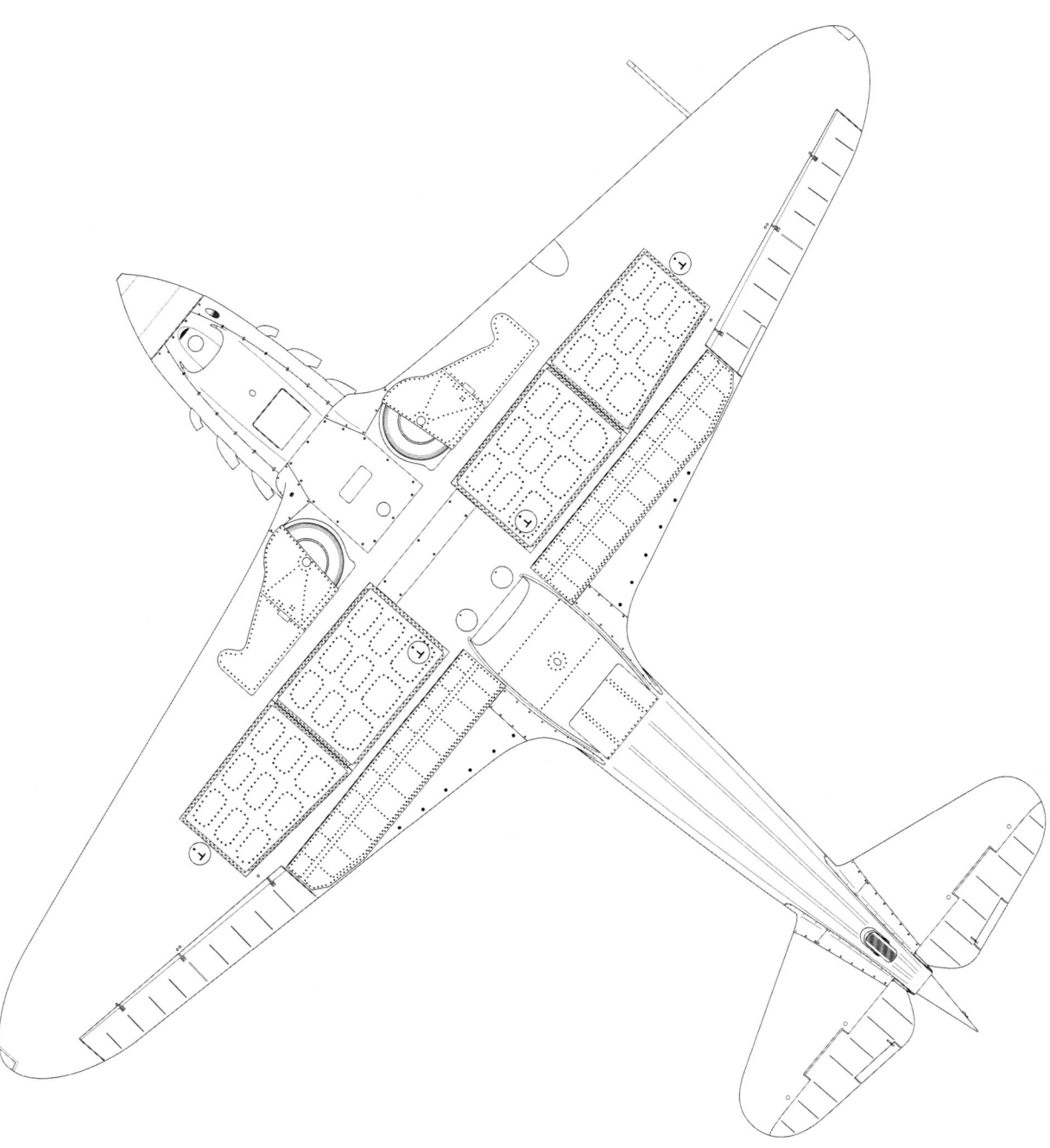

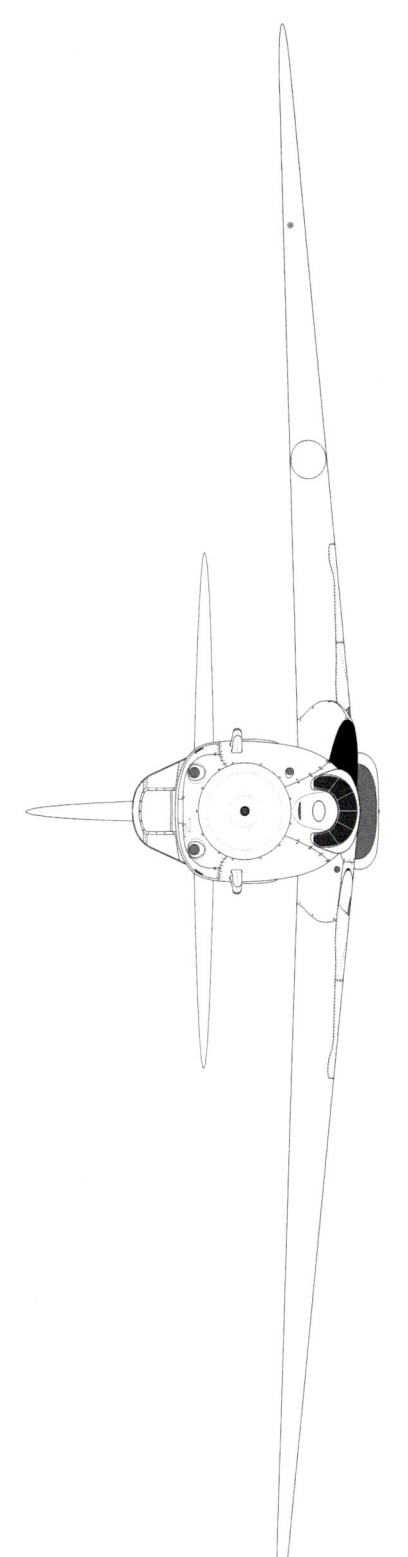

Engine:
- *Klimov M-105P, 1050 hp for take-off & emergency*

Armament:
- *2 x 7.62 mm ShKAS machine-guns (synchronised) with 750 rds per gun*
- *1 x 20 mm ShVAK cannon firing through spinner with 110 rounds*

Yak-1 Series 20 *Massovii*, Factory № 292

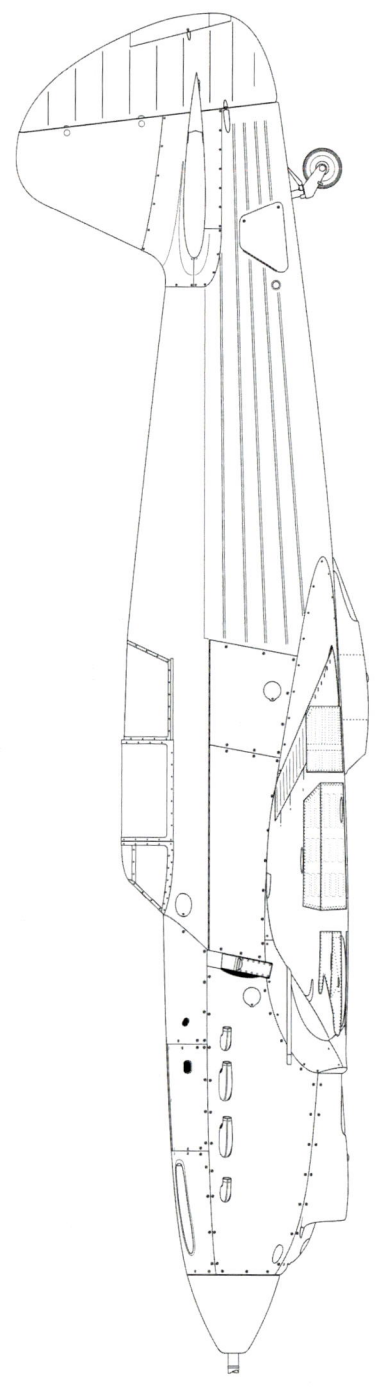

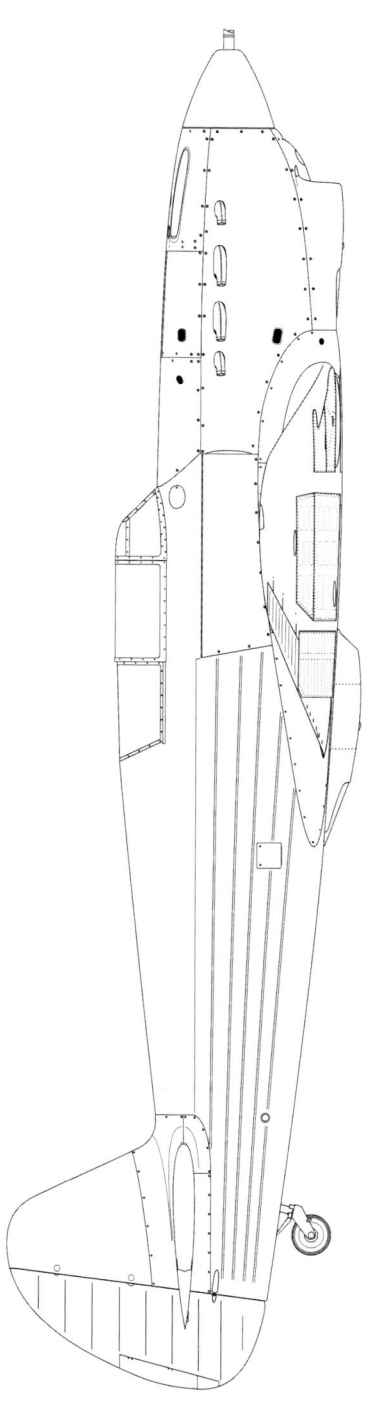

Main Feature Changes:

- *Single piece Saratov style spinner with long Hucks collar*
- *Revised port wing root intake*
- *Many internal detail and systems changes*

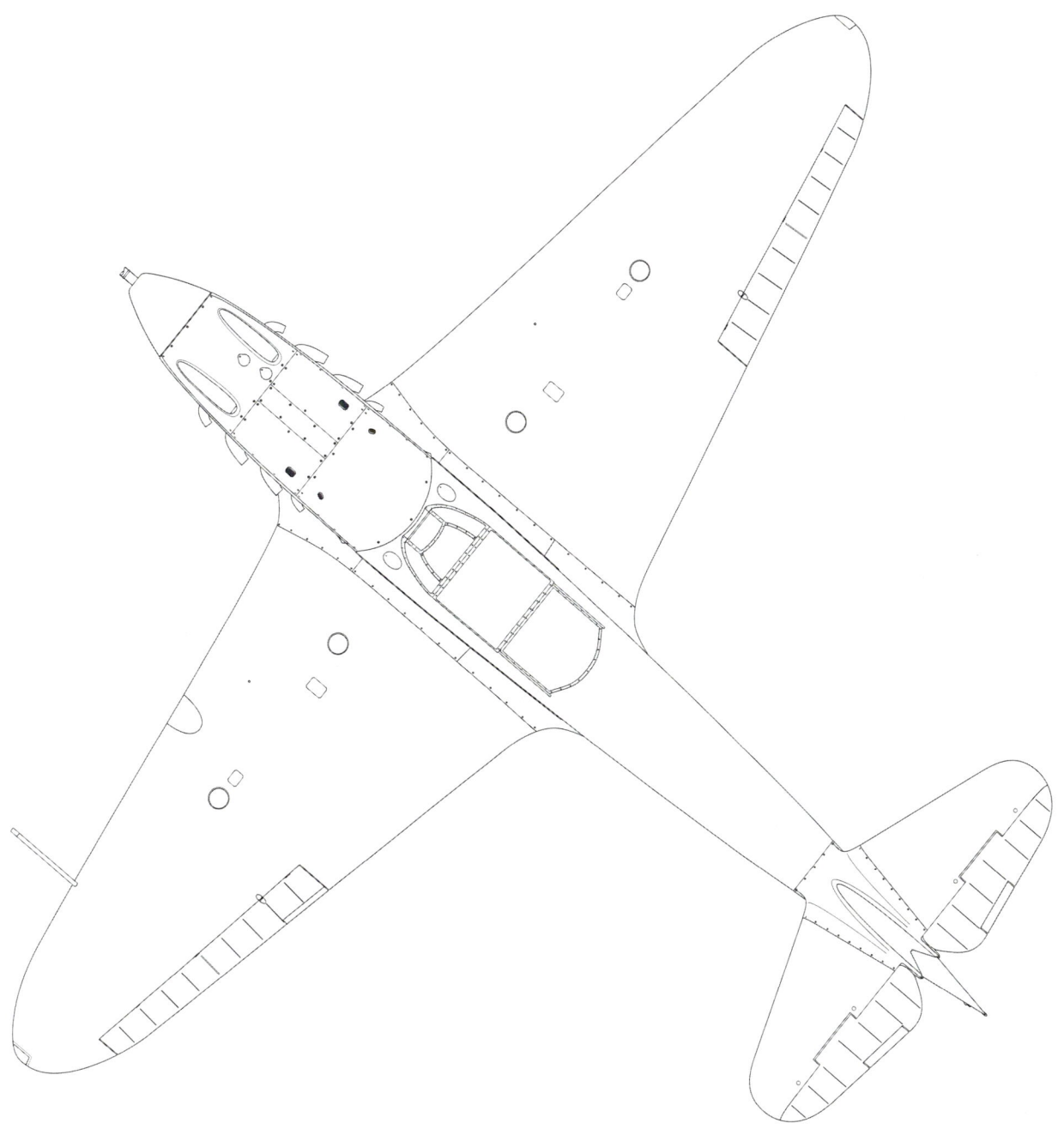

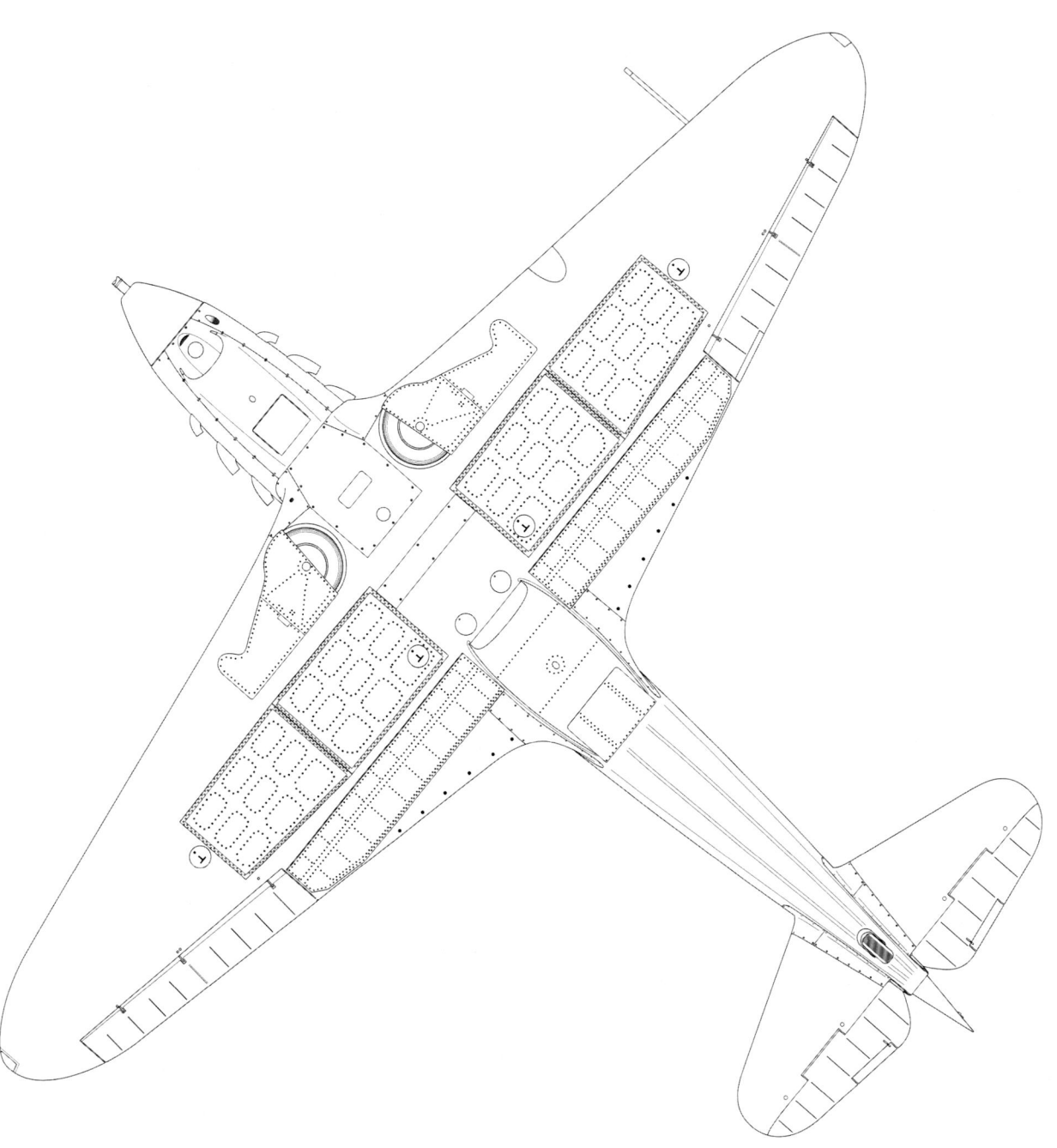

Engine:
- *Klimov M-105PA, 1100 hp for take-off & emergency*

Armament:
- *2 x 7.62 mm ShKAS machine-guns (synchronised) with 750 rds per gun*
- *1 x 20 mm ShVAK cannon firing through spinner with 120 rounds*

Yak-1 *2 x UBS*, Factory № 292

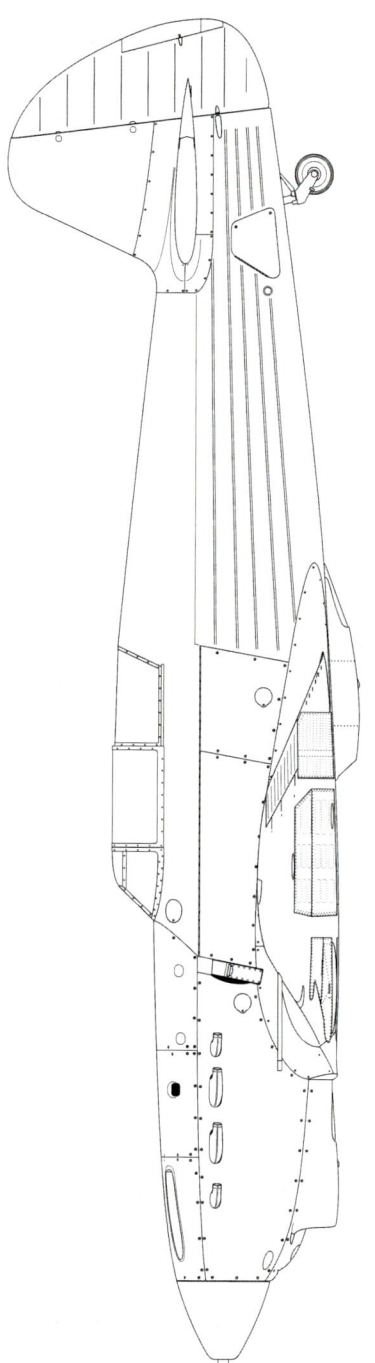

By 1941 there was increasing concern over the hitting power of rifle calibre guns, to include the 7.62 mm ShKAS (despite its otherwise excellent performance). Many armament changes, schemes and plans were devolved during this time by the government and its related Ministries. Pertinent to these activities, an unknown number of Yak-1s were built roughly somewhere between Series 20 and 40 with two Berezin UBS guns replacing the existing ShKAS (even Stepanets does not have the exact details).

It is likely that the UBS guns were fitted with the same ammunition casettes as the later Yak-7B (with a total of 400 rounds), and the ShVAK might have been supplied with either 110 or 120 cartridges, depending upon the Series of the aircraft so modified.

Main Feature Changes:
- *Revised upper cowling with gun bulges and modified link and gas ports*

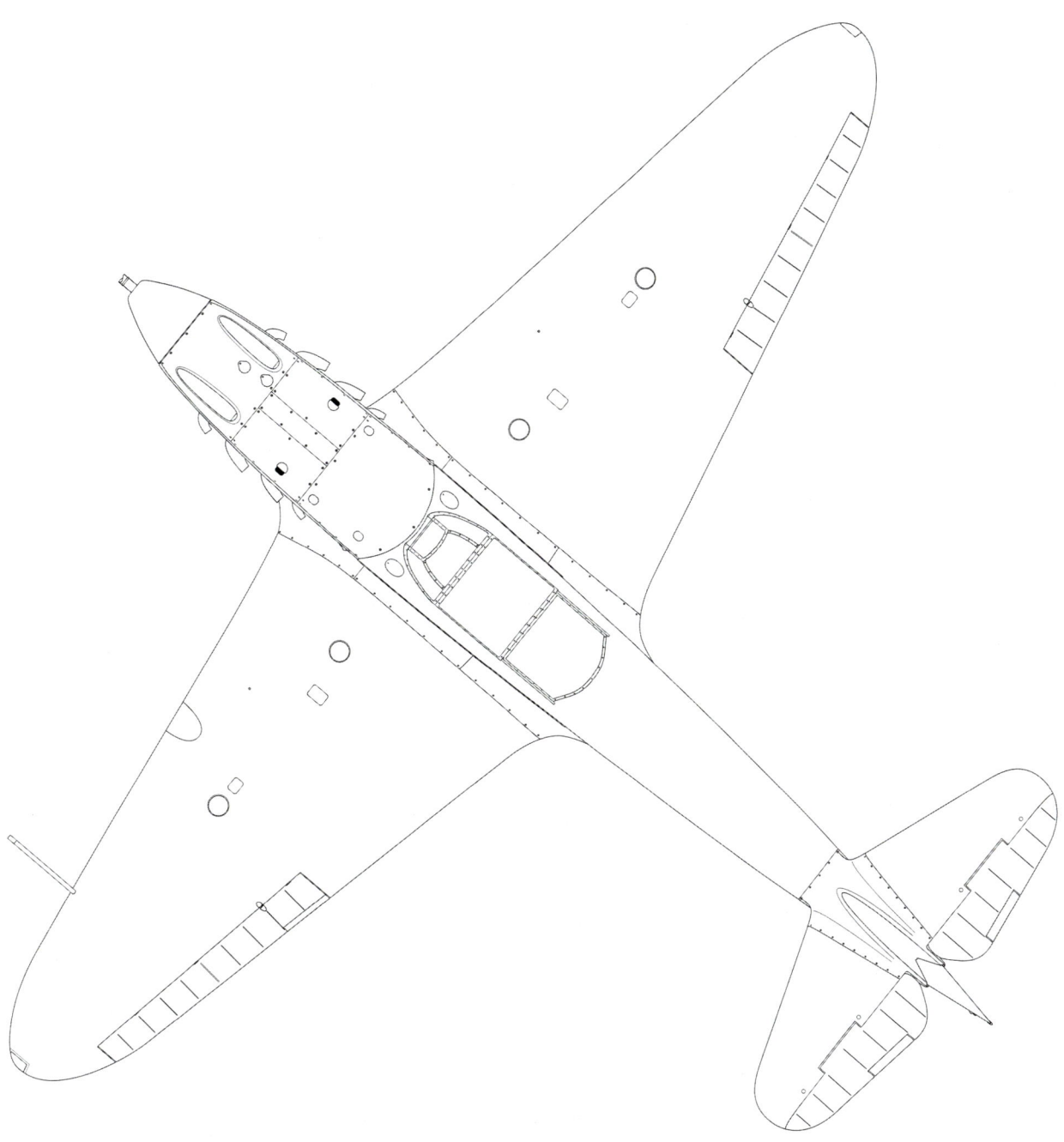

Yak-1 Series 43, Factory № 292

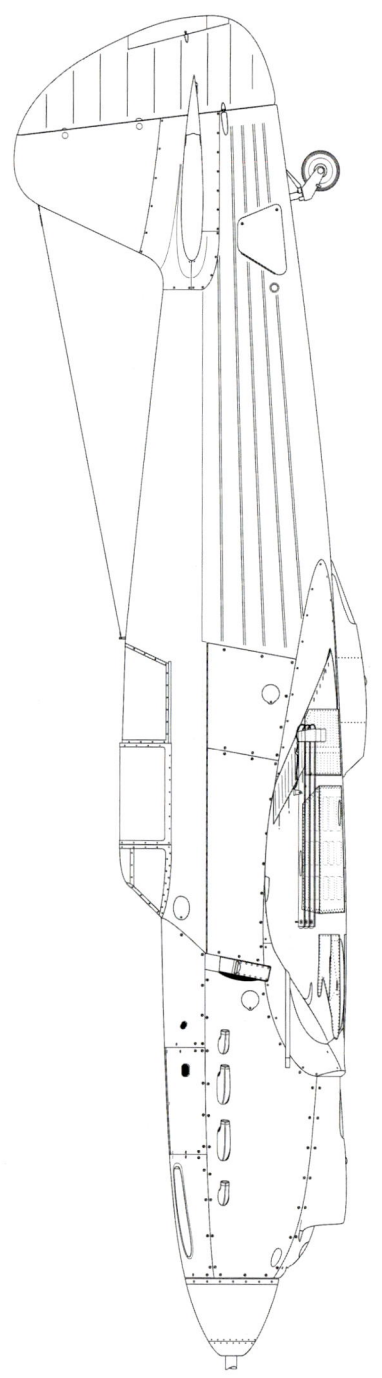

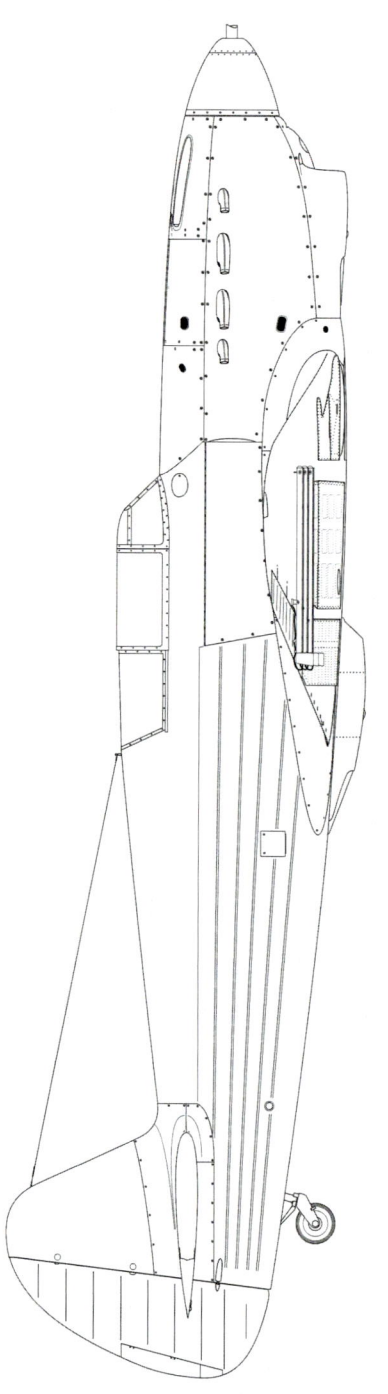

Main Feature Changes:

- *Revised two piece spinner with shorter Hucks collar*
- *Radio stub dipole fitting and RSI-4 unit increasingly common*
- *Six RO82 rocket rails mounted under outer wing surfaces*

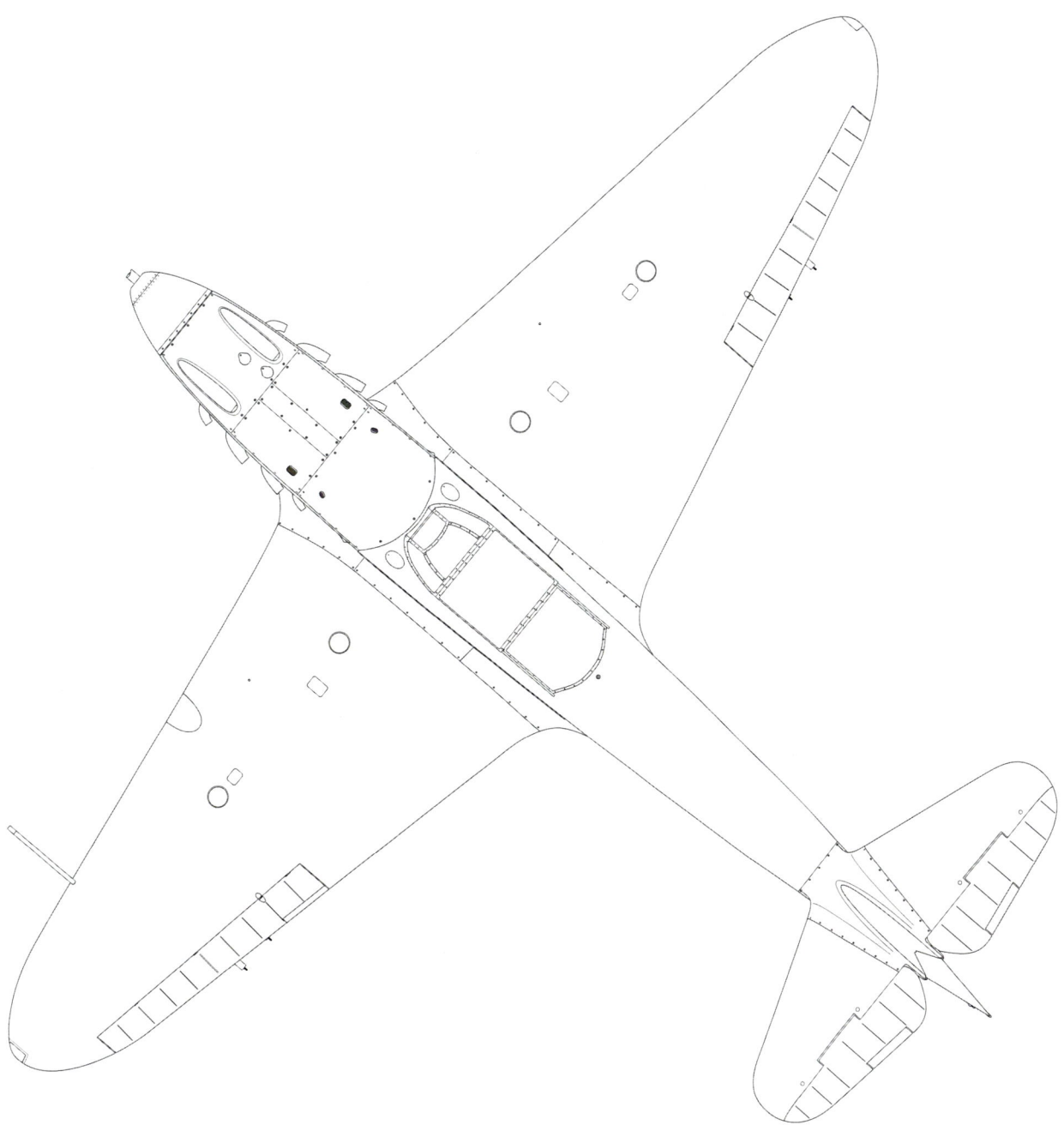

Scrap view of rocket installation from below **1:48 scale**

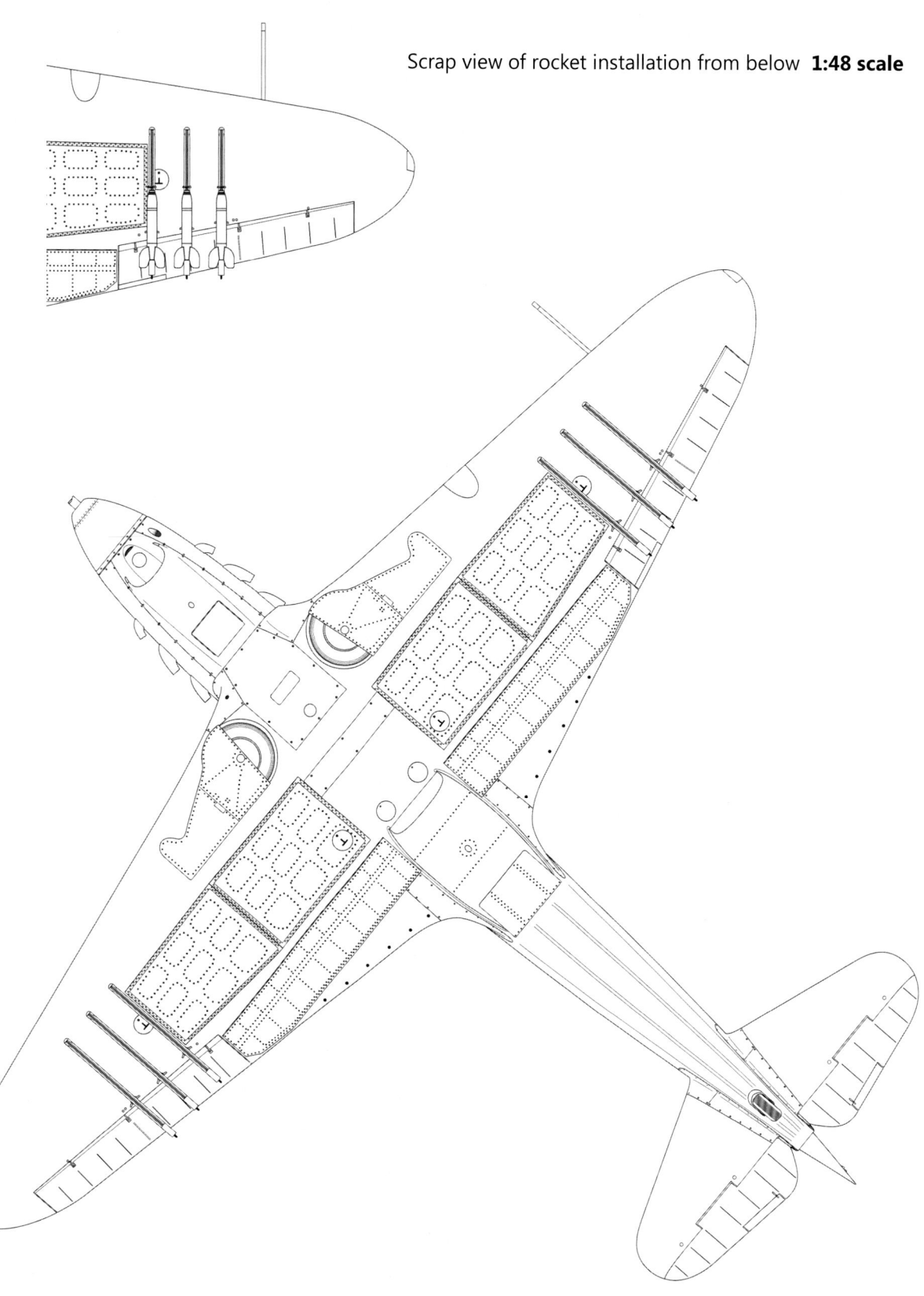

Engine:
- *Klimov M-105PA, 1100 hp for take-off & emergency*

Armament:
- *2 x 7.62 mm ShKAS machine-guns (synchronised) with 750 rds per gun*
- *1 x 20 mm ShVAK cannon firing through spinner with 120 rounds*
- *6 x RS-82 rockets*

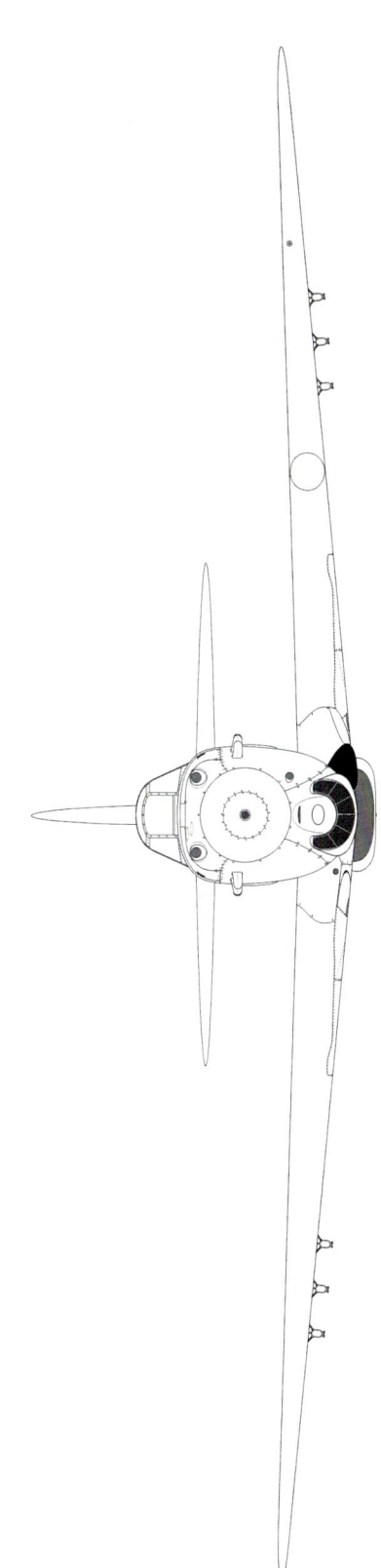

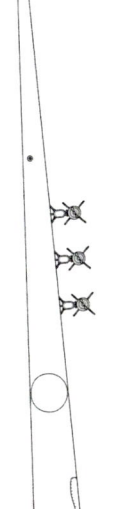

Scrap view of rocket installation from front   **1:48 scale**

Yak-1 Series 49, Factory № 292

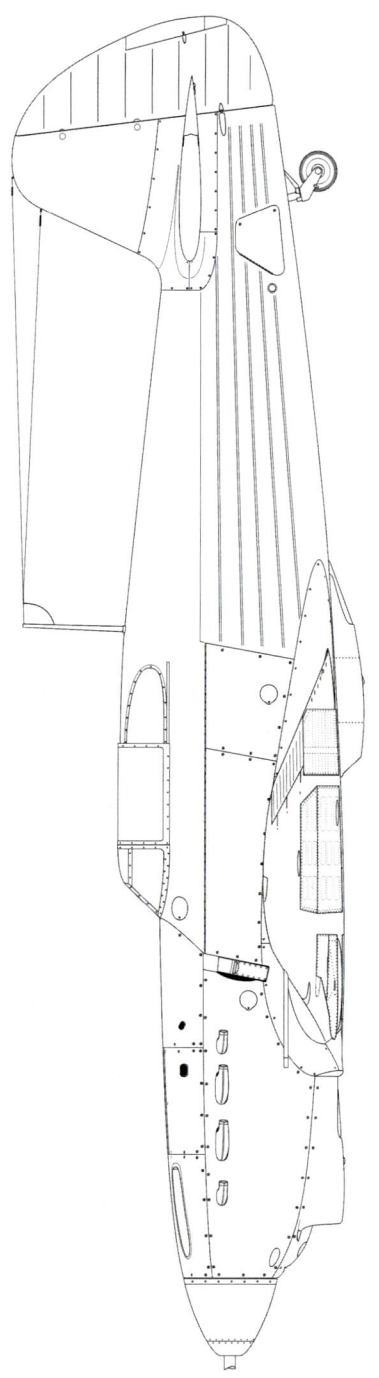
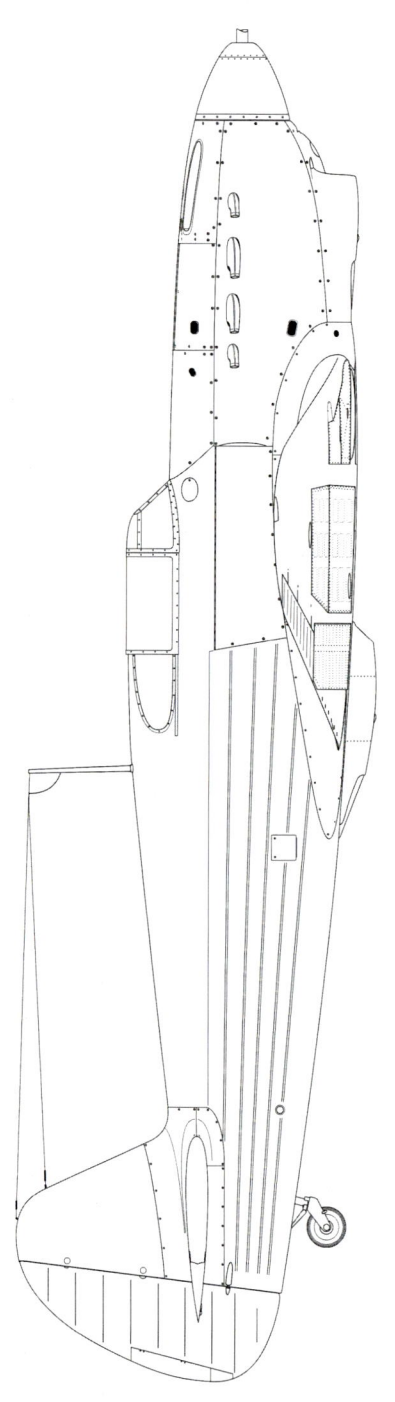

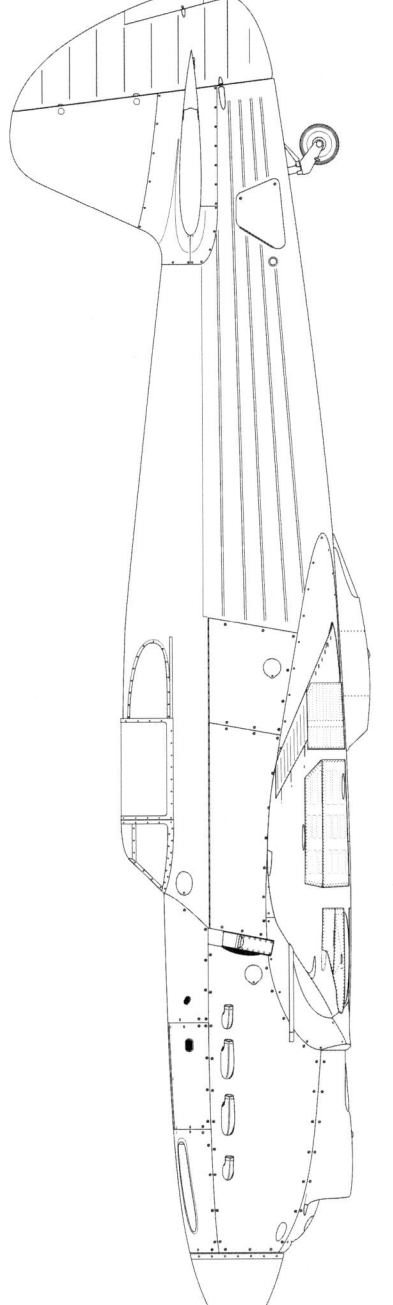

Earlier example lacking a radio mast, as delivered by the factory. Some units in the field also removed the radio mast, giving a similar appearance.

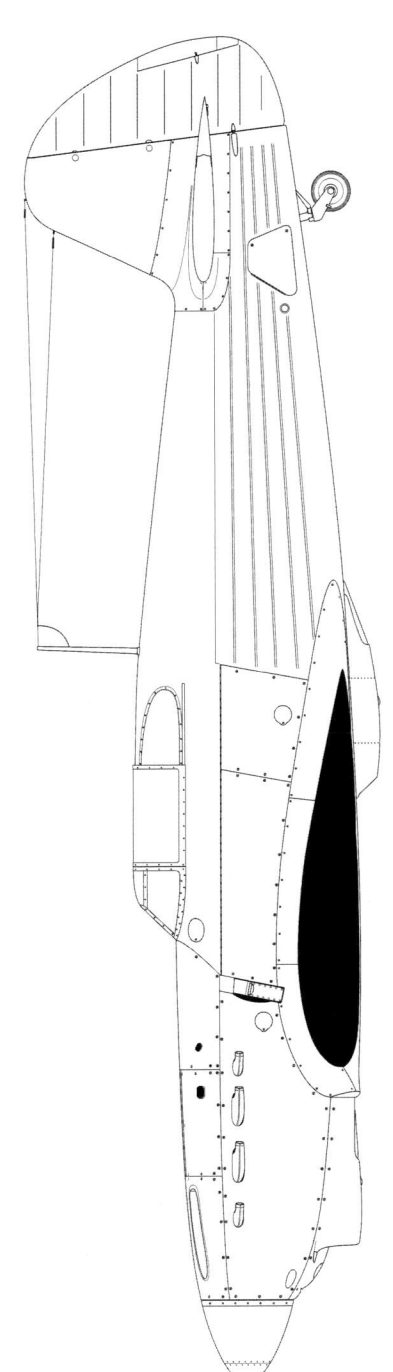

Port side view with the wing removed showing the wing root fillet detail. The aerofoil at the root was **Clark YH 15.15** %.

Engine:
- *Klimov M-105PA, 1100 hp for take-off & emergency*
- *From Series 85 M-105PF, 1260 hp for take-off & emergency*

Armament:
- *2 x 7.62 mm ShKAS machine-guns (synchronised) with 750 rds per gun*
- *1 x 20 mm ShVAK cannon firing through spinner with 120 rounds*

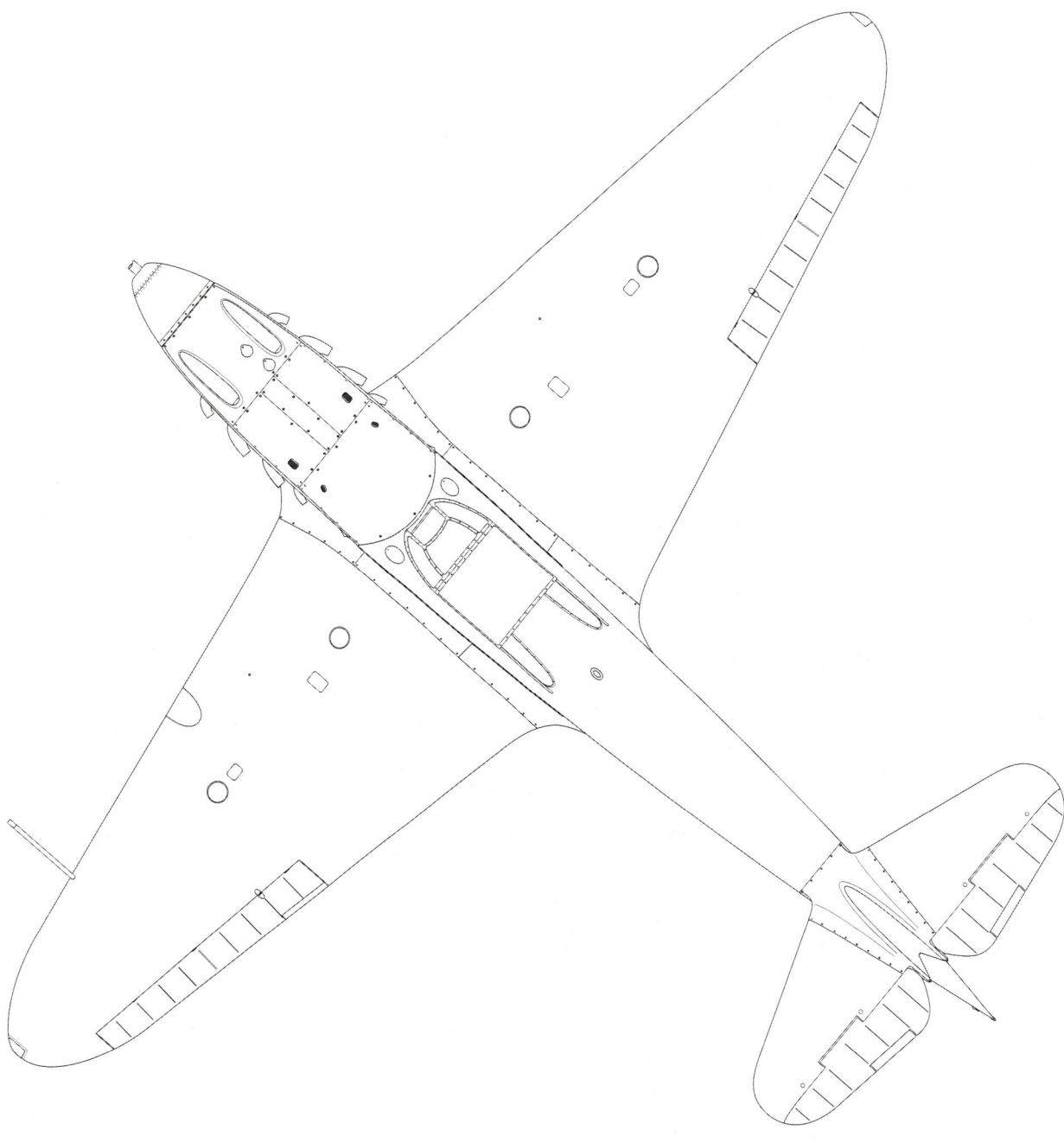

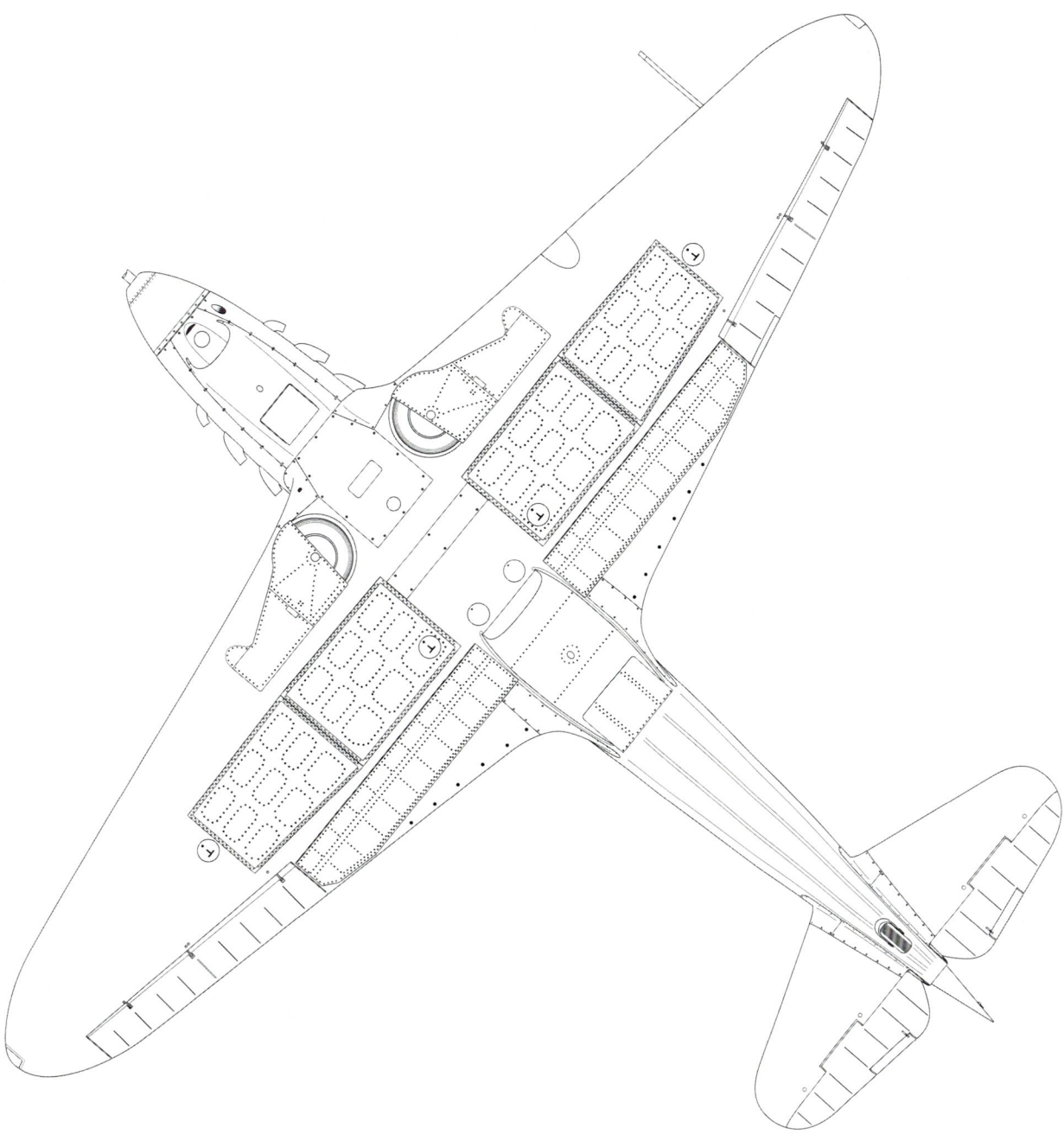

Main Feature Changes:

- *Aft clear canopy section replaced with two half-round windows*
- *Large radio mast and aerials installed when fitted with RSI-4*
- *Revised main gear door shape at the pivot joint*

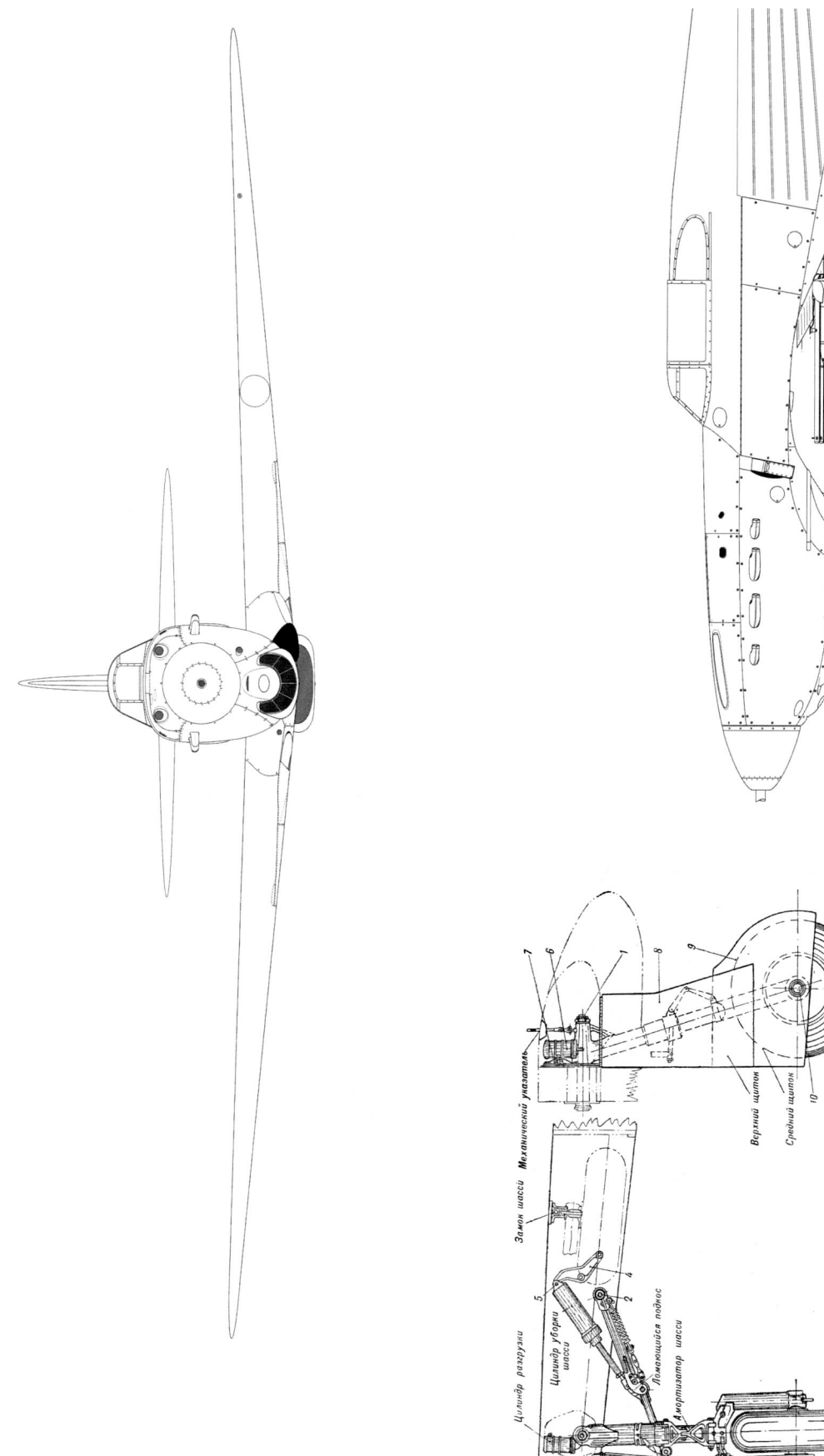

Some of the earliest examples (Series 49 to 54) were armed with six RS-82 rockets. Here the missiles are shown in place on the RO82 rails. [1:48 scale]

A superb illustration of the Series 49 landing gear from the Yak-1 *Tekhnicheskoe Opisanie* (Technical Manual).

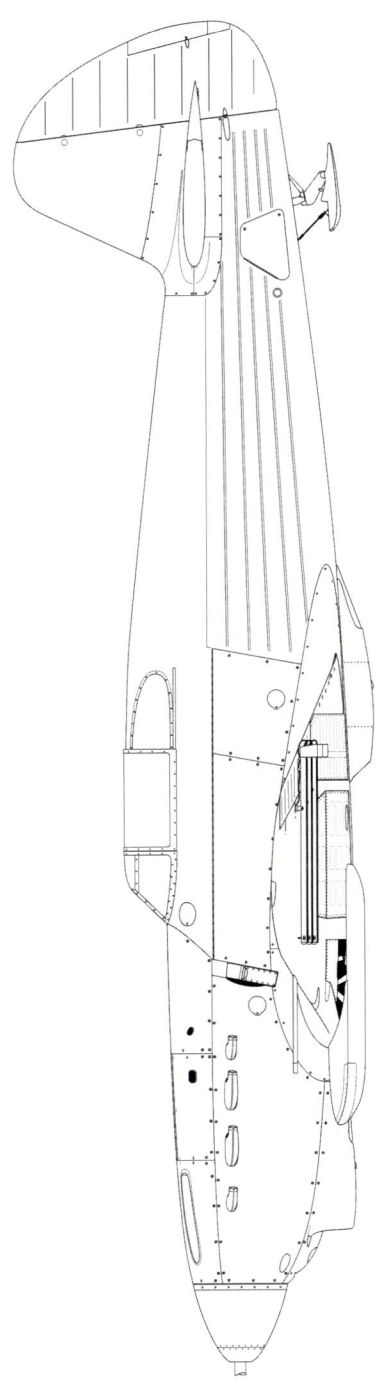

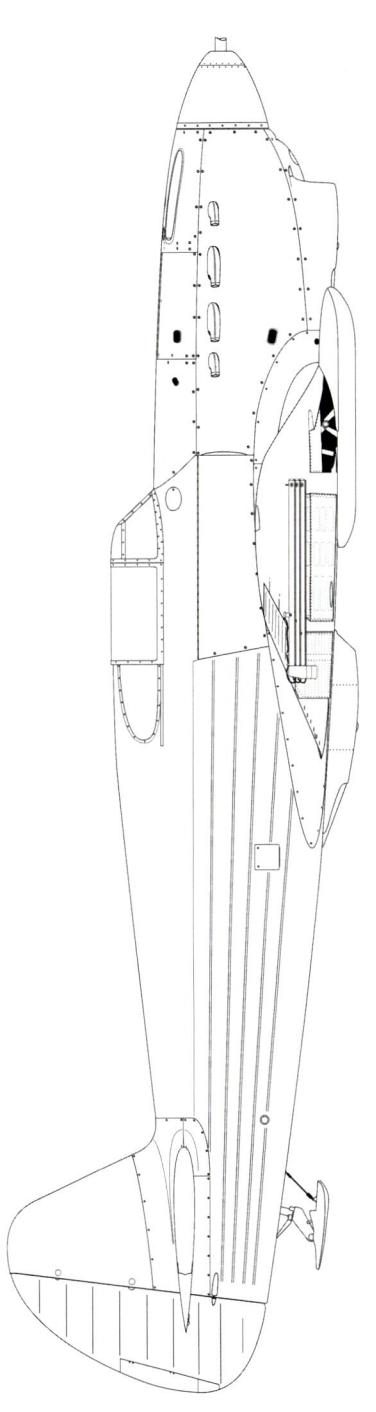

Main Feature Changes:

- *Main landing gear tyres replaced by ski units*
- *End portion of main gear door removed to accommodate skis*
- *Tail wheel replaced by ski unit*

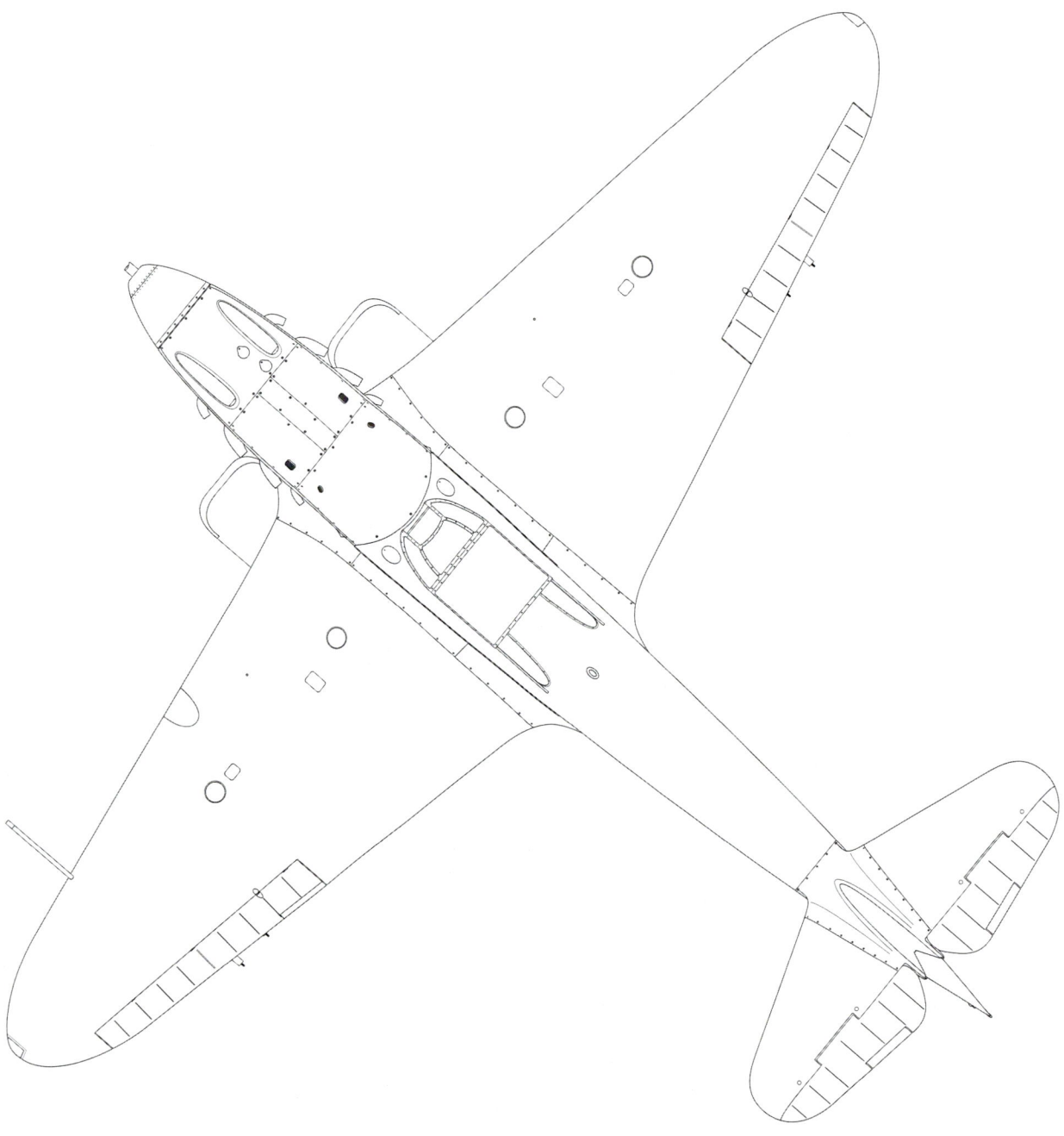

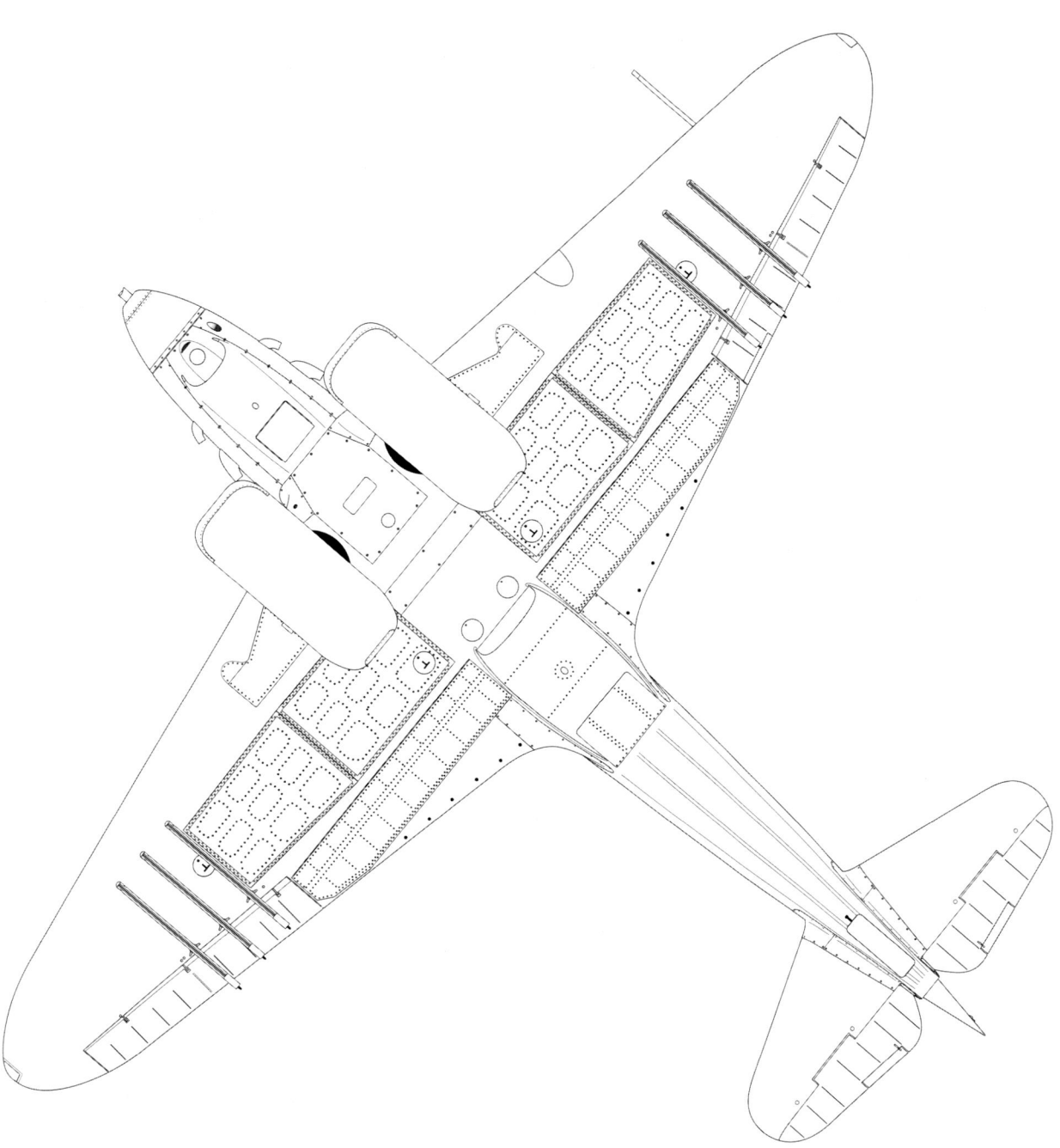

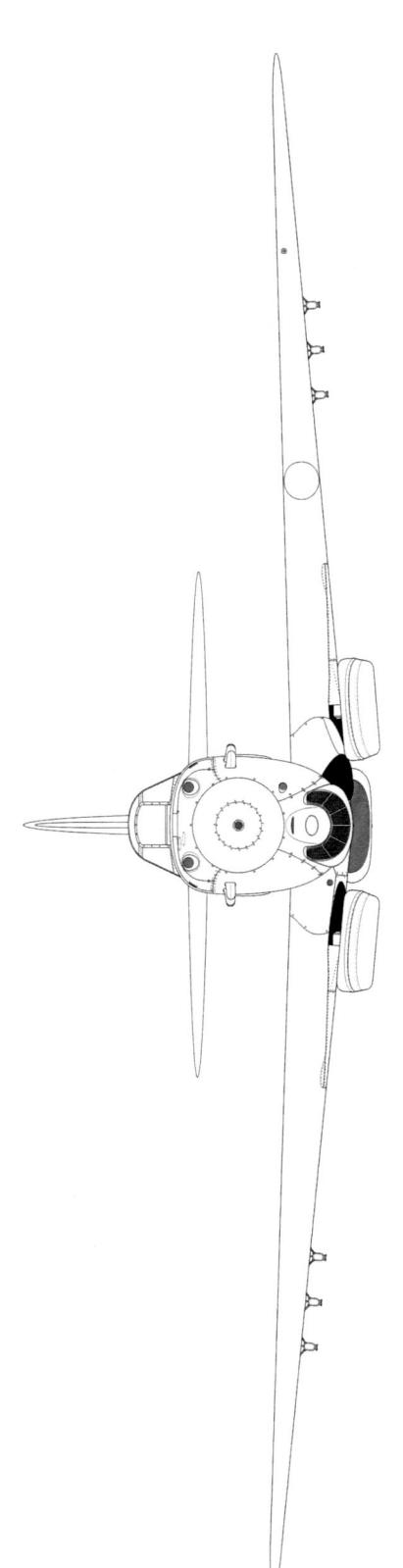

Engine:
* *Klimov M-105PA, 1100 hp for take-off & emergency*

Armament:
* *2 x 7.62 mm ShKAS machine-guns (synchronised) with 750 rds per gun*
* *1 x 20 mm ShVAK cannon firing through spinner with 120 rounds*
* *6 x RS-82 rockets*

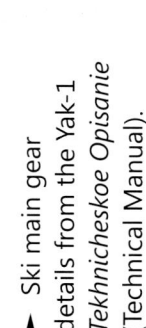
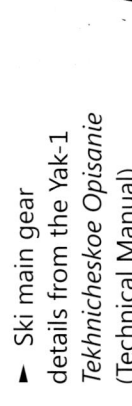

Рис. 63. Установка лыжи

▶ Ski main gear details from the Yak-1 *Tekhnicheskoe Opisanie* (Technical Manual).

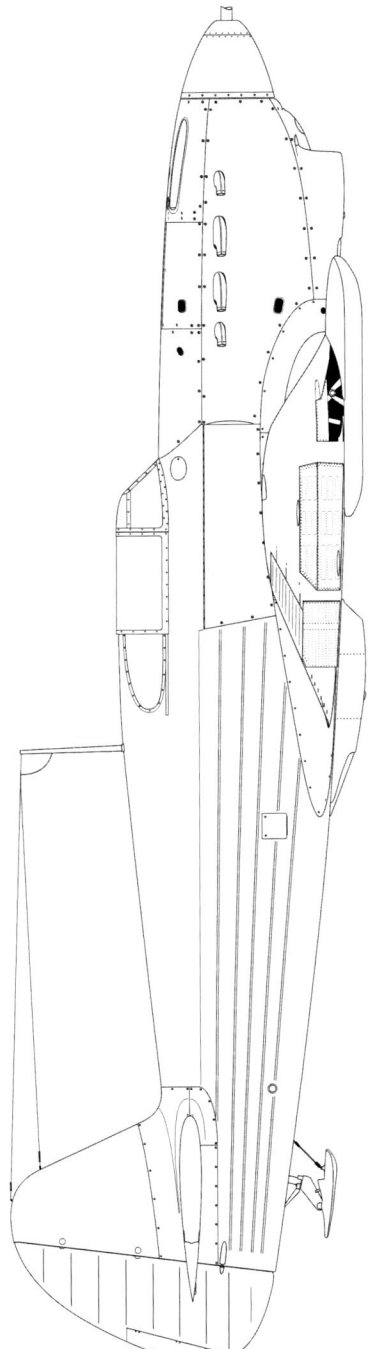

Increasingly, Yak-1s were completed at the factory with RSI-4 radios and associated mast and aerials and no rocket armament. Here is a winterised *massovii* with these changess (starboard view).

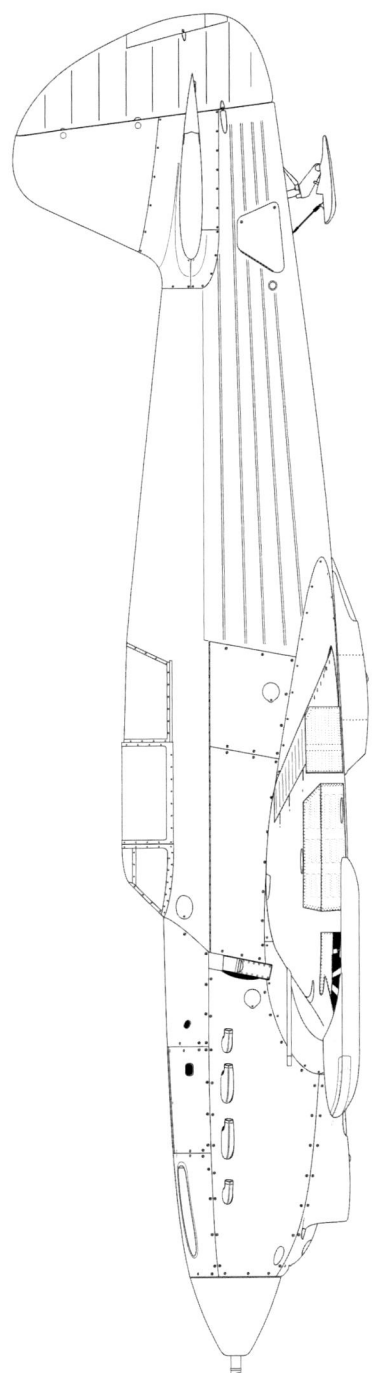

Port view of a pre-*massovii* winterised aircraft, ca, Series 40.

Yak-1 Series 90, Factory № 292

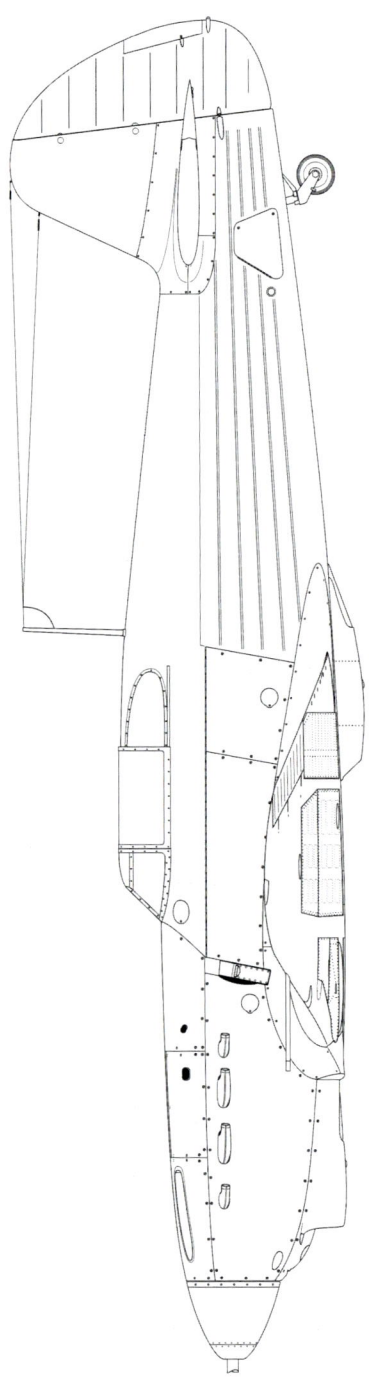

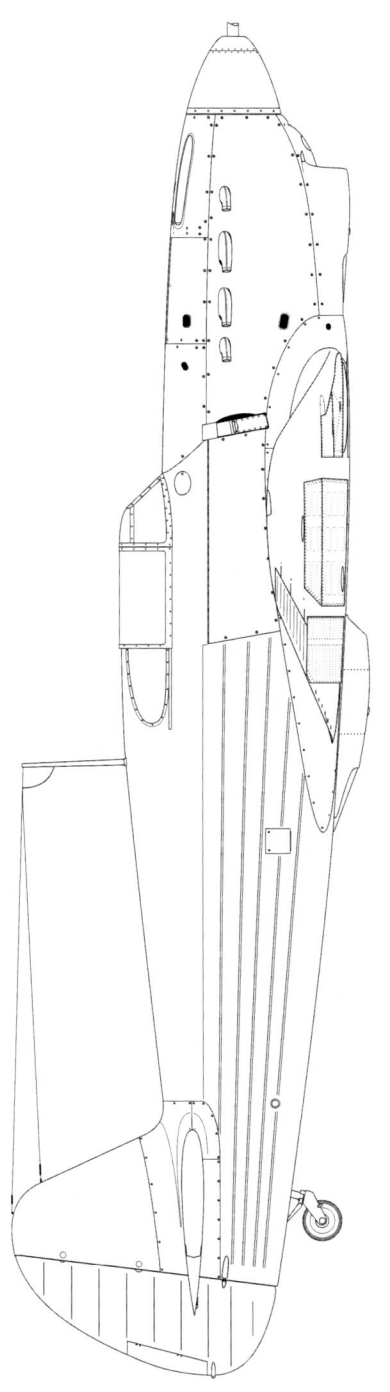

Main Feature Changes:
- *Ammunition cassette access added to starboard side of nose*
- *Revised rudder navigation lamp*

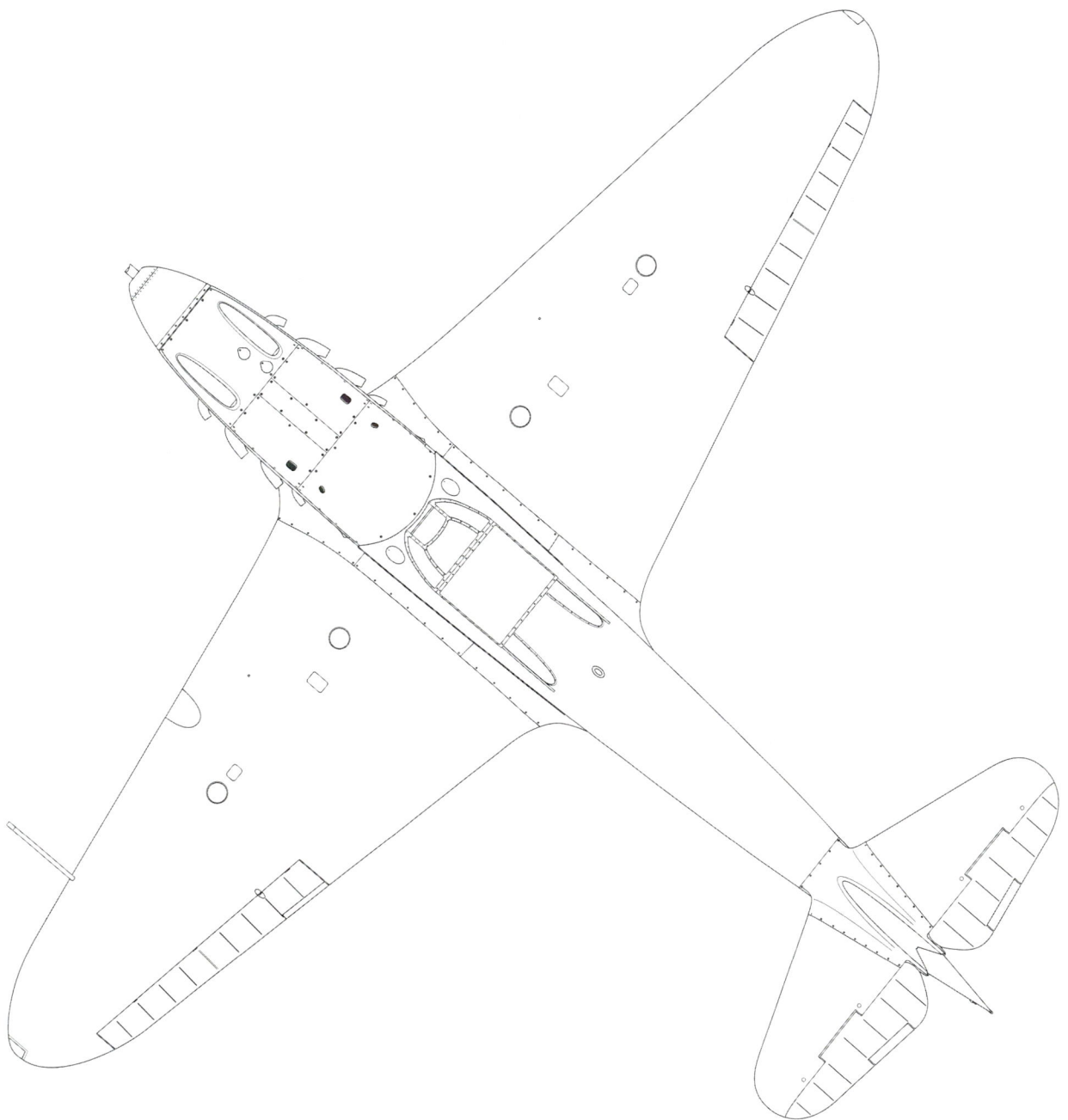

Engine:
- *Klimov M-105PF, 1260 hp for take-off & emergency*

Armament:
- *2 x 7.62 mm ShKAS machine-guns (synchronised) with 750 rds per gun*
- *1 x 20 mm ShVAK cannon firing through spinner with 120 rounds*

Yak-1 *Oblegchennyi* Series 96, Factory № 292

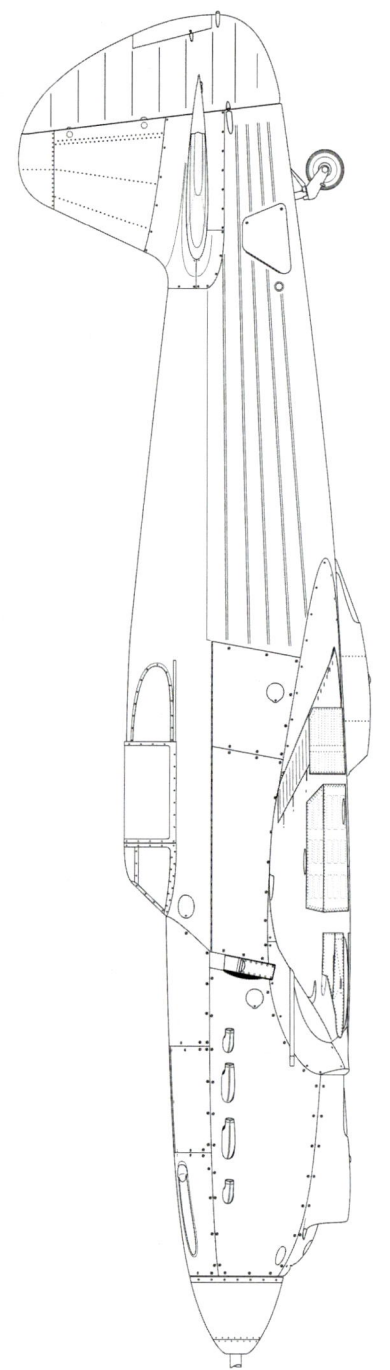

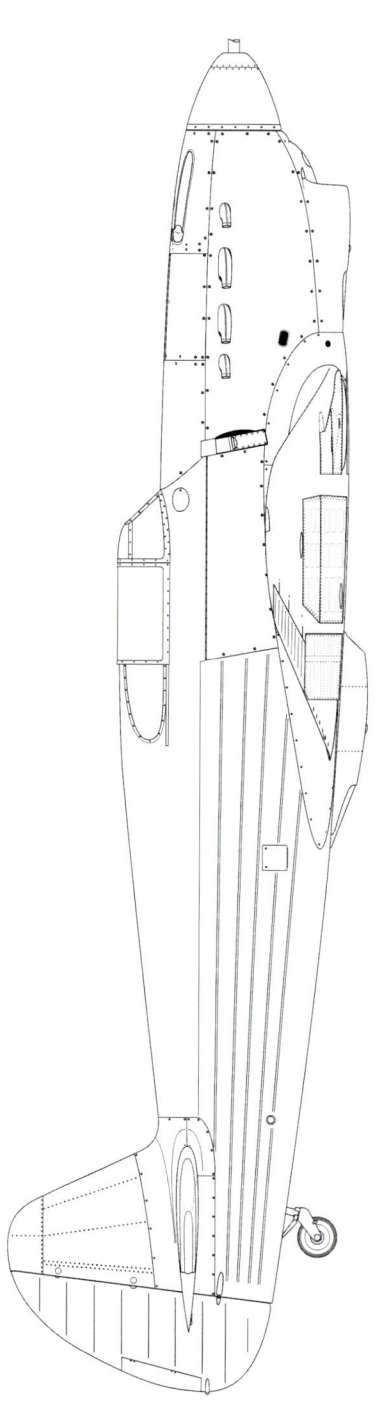

Main Feature Changes:
- *All-metal stabilisers and fin from Yak-7*
- *Radio, mast, aerials and ShKAS guns removed*
- *Gun ports, links chute and gas exit closed with covers*

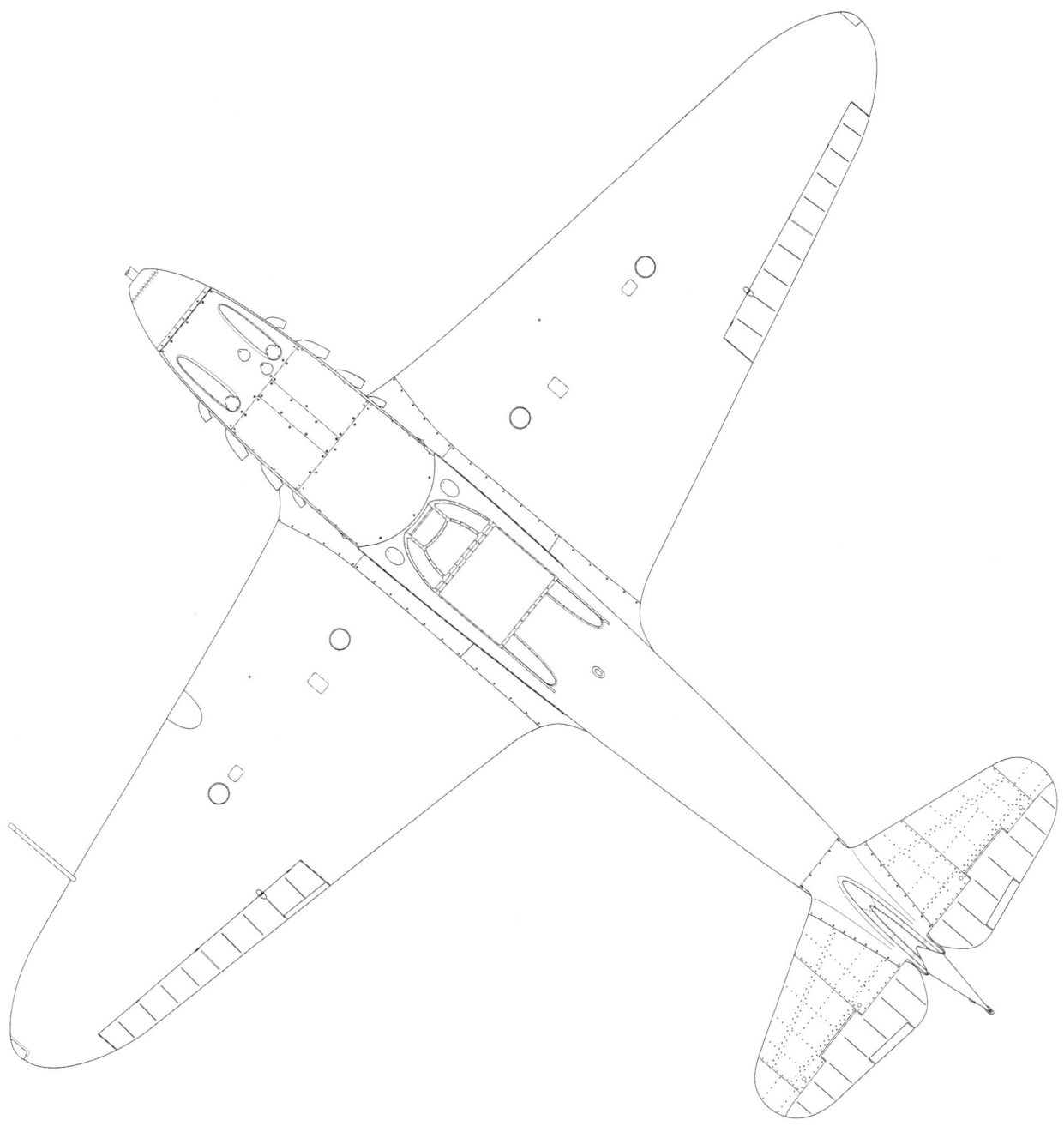

Engine:
- *Klimov M-105PF, 1260 hp for take-off & emergency*

Armament:
- *1 x 20 mm ShVAK cannon firing through spinner with 120 rounds*

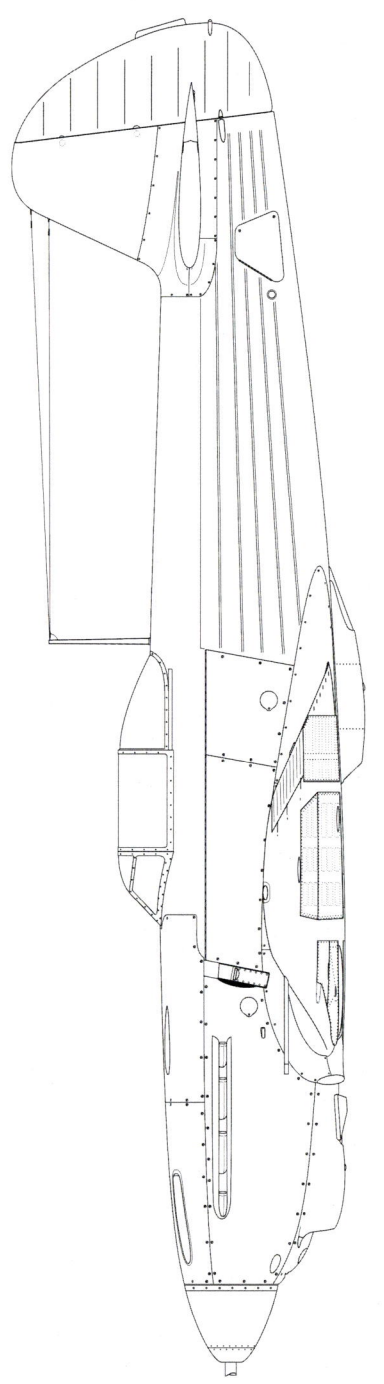

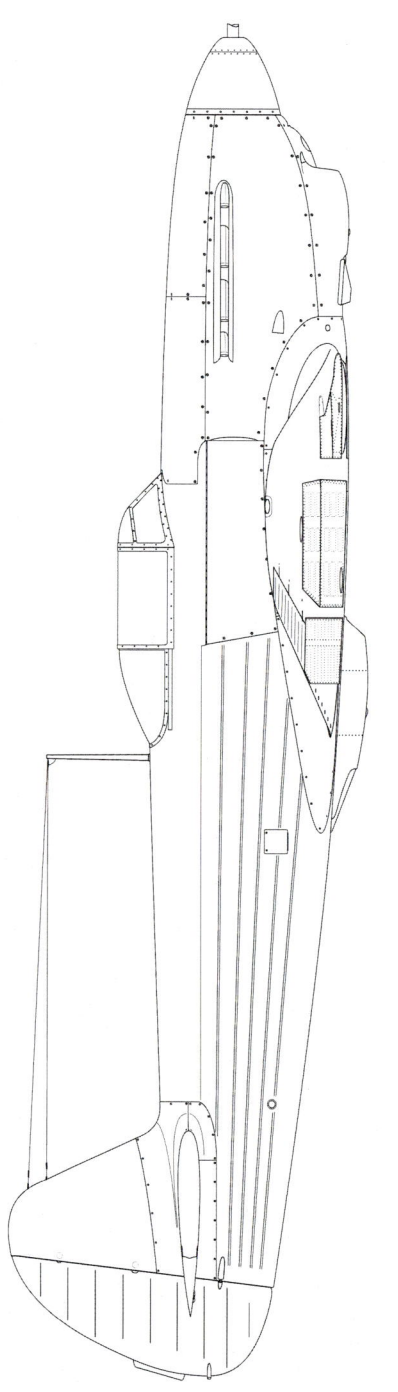

Main Feature Changes:
- *Cut-down rear fuselage with shaped clear cockpit section*
- *Single gun in upper cowling (port side) with blister*
- *Revised port wing root intake*
- *Wing leading edge landing light removed*
- *Armoured windscreen*
- *Ground adjustable aileron and rudder trim tabs*
- *Fully retractable tail wheel*
- *New cowling panels and details*
- *Exhaust stack fillet*

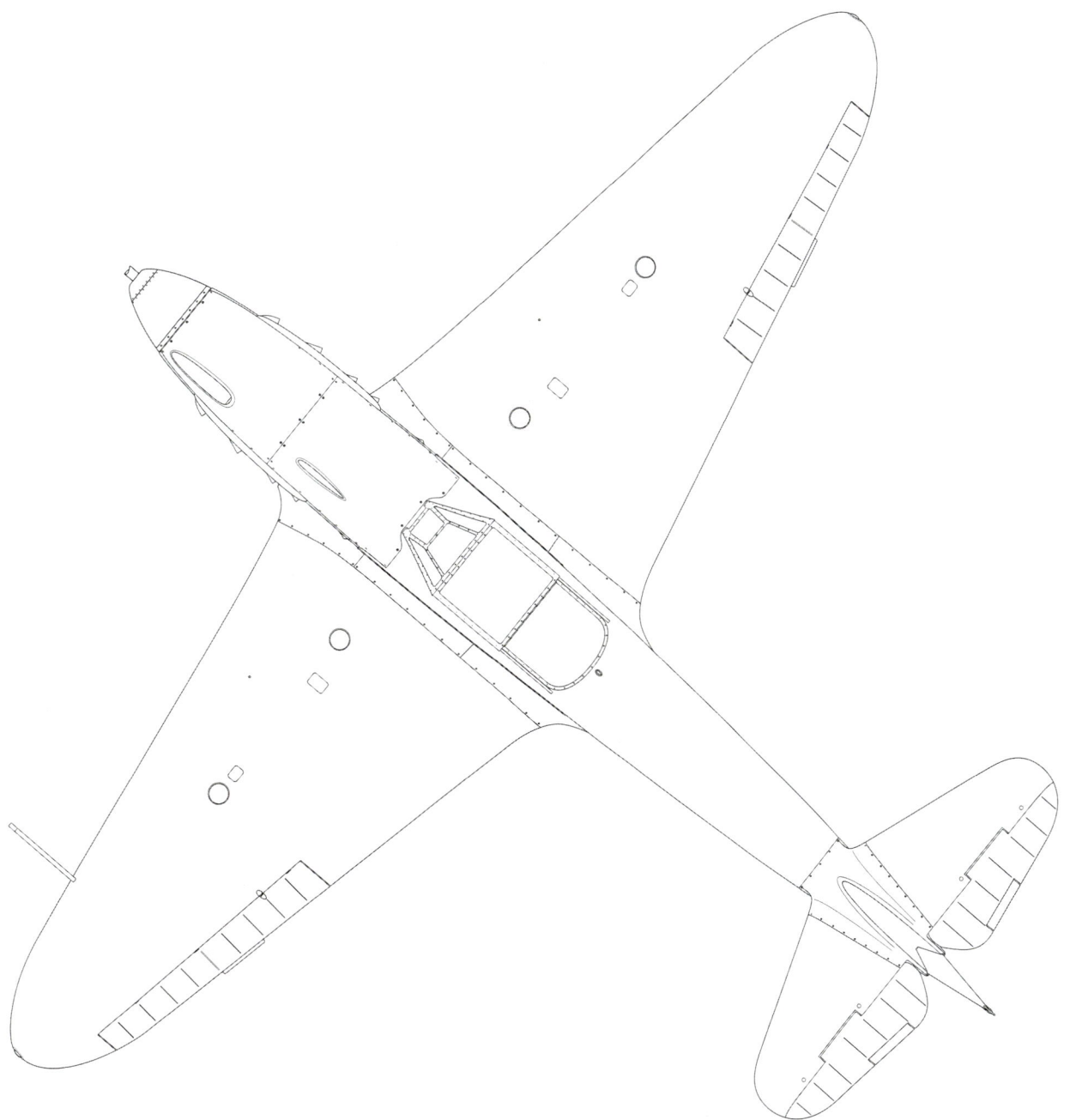

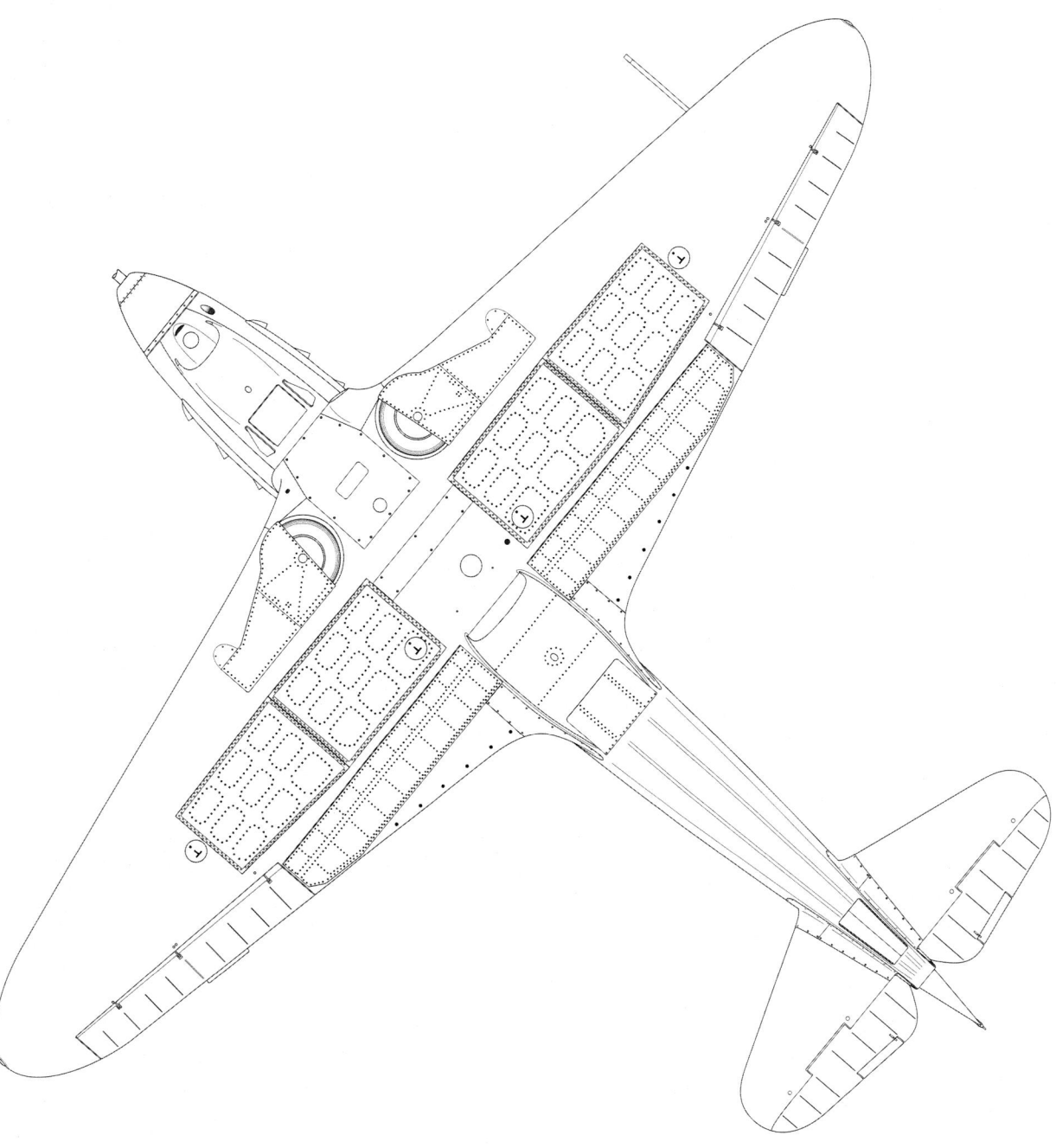

Engine:
- *Klimov M-105PF, 1260 hp for take-off & emergency*

Armament:
- *1 x 12.7 mm UBS machine-gun (synchronised) with 200 rds per gun*
- *1 x 20 mm ShVAK cannon firing through spinner with 120 rounds*

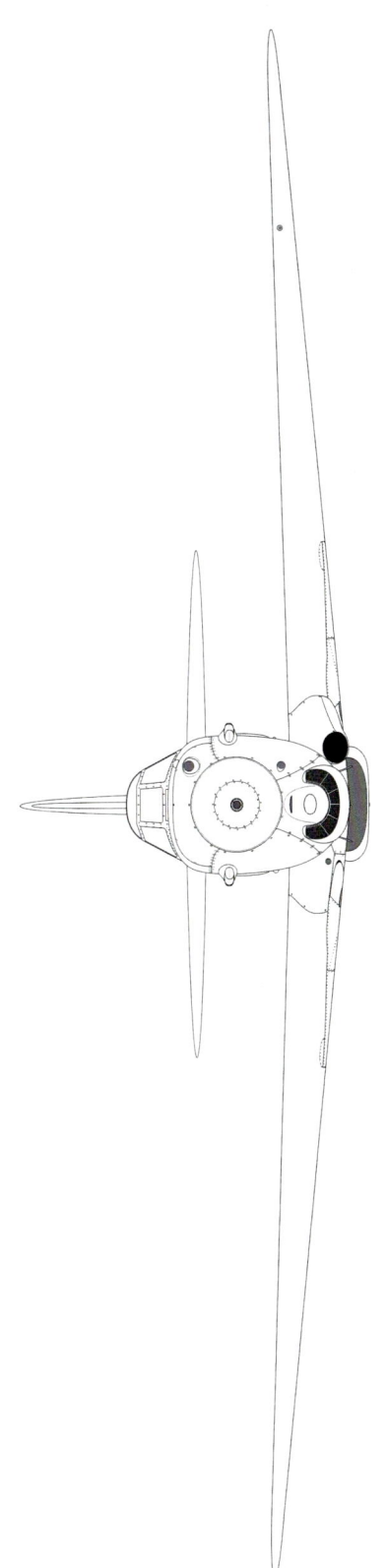

Yak-1B *Massovii* (UA) Series 111, Factory № 292

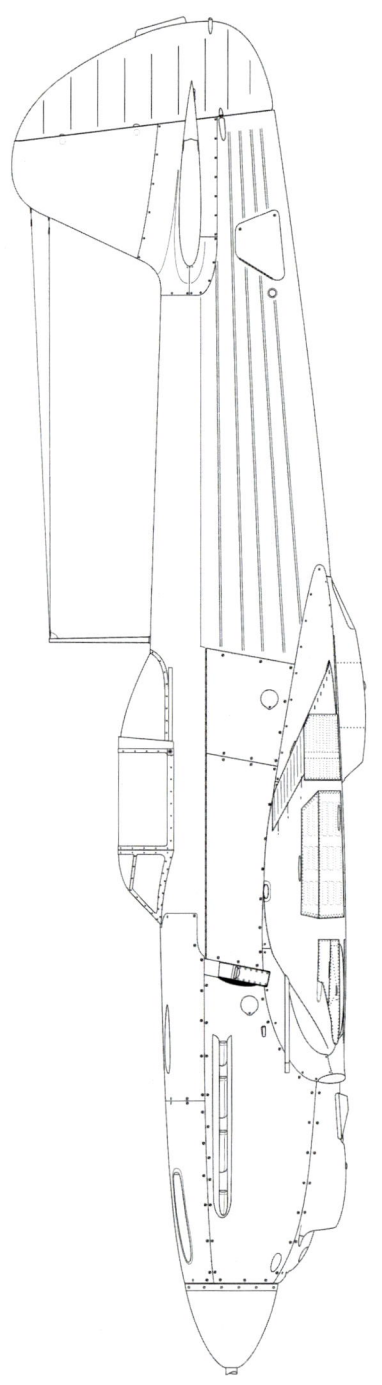
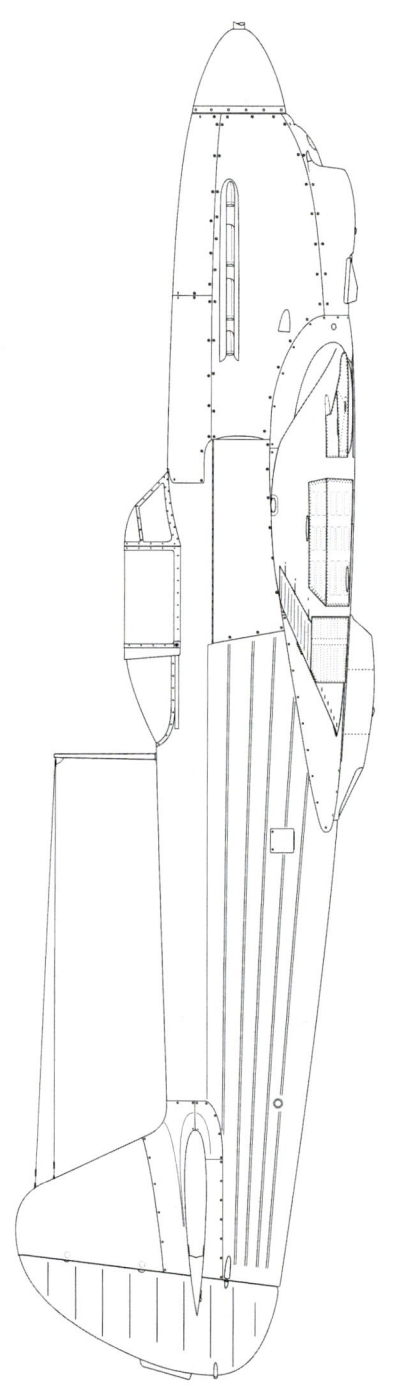

Main Feature Changes:

- *Revised elevator shape*
- *Improved aileron connection fairings*
- *Revised radiator outlet door*
- *Sliding canopy aft edge fairing*
- *New streamlined one piece spinner*

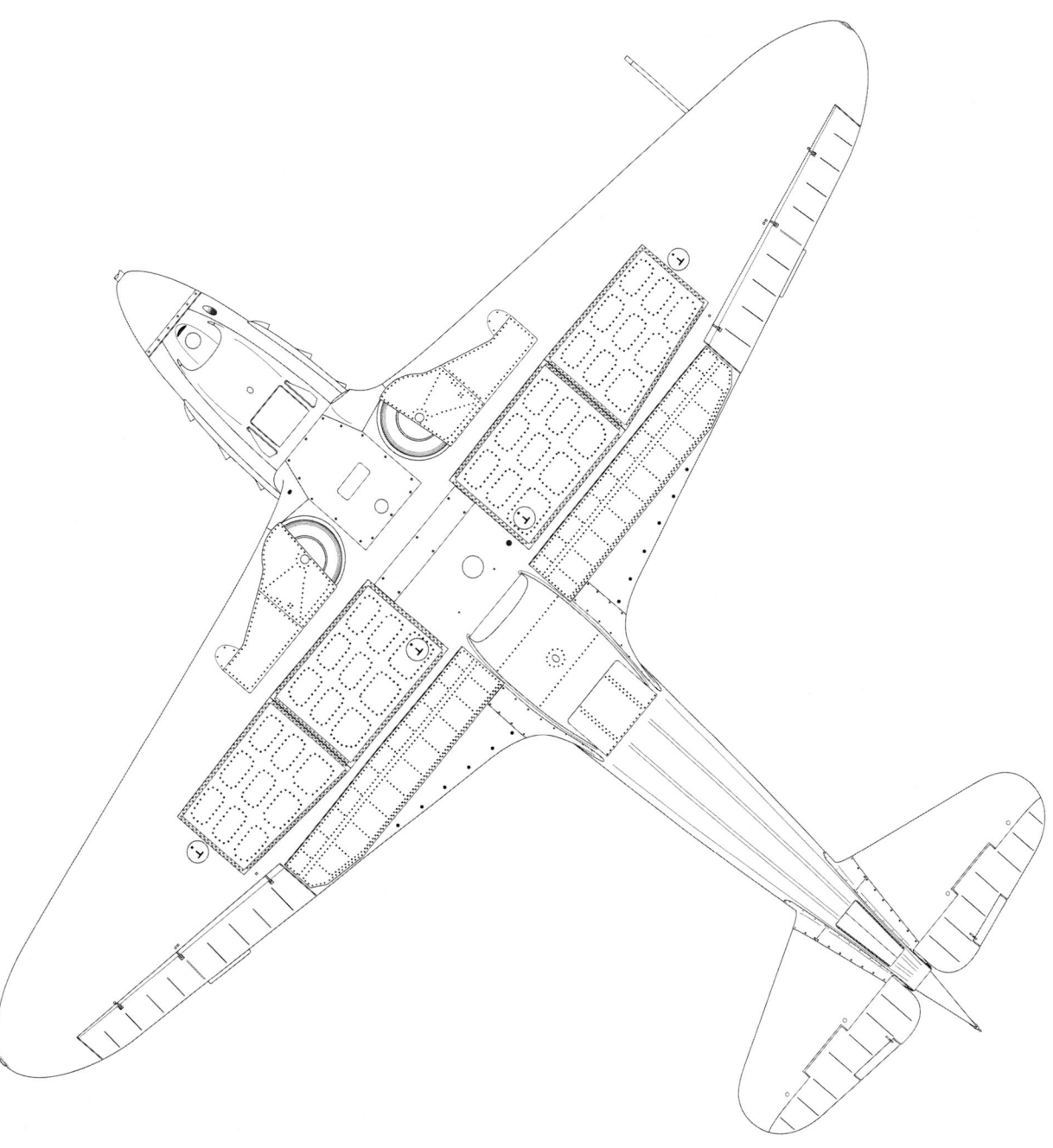

Yak-1B *Oblegchennyi* Series 127-147, Factory № 292

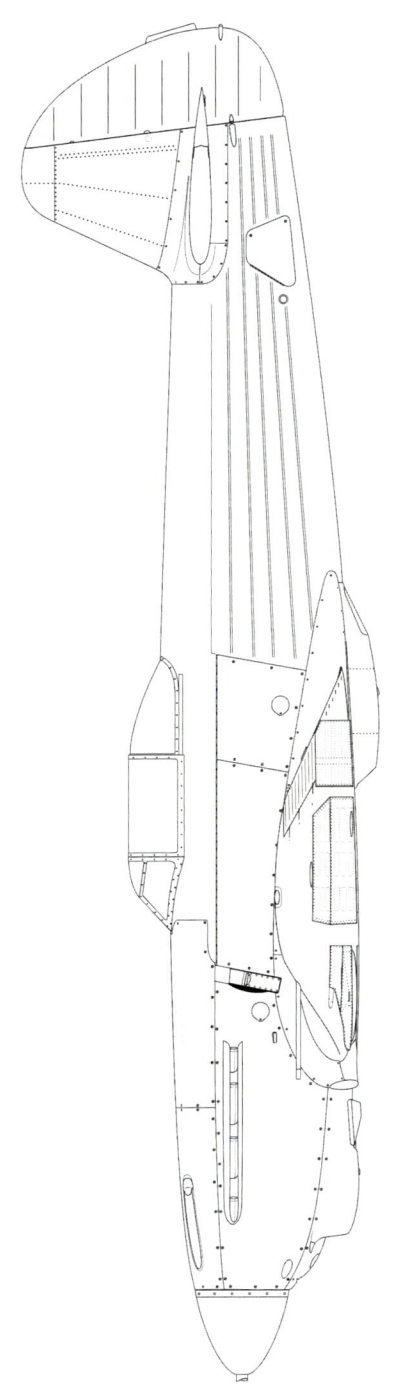

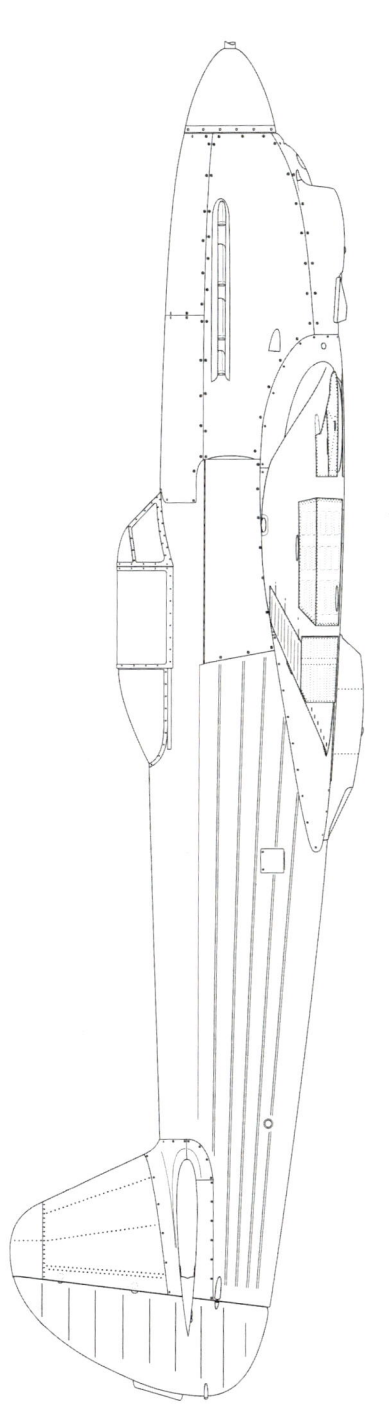

Main Feature Changes:

- *"Yak-3" style stabilisers from the Yak-1M 'dubler' prototype*
- *Radio, mast, aerials and UBS gun removed*
- *Gun port closed with cover*
- *"Yak-7" type metal fin*
- *Sliding canopy aft extension usually omitted*

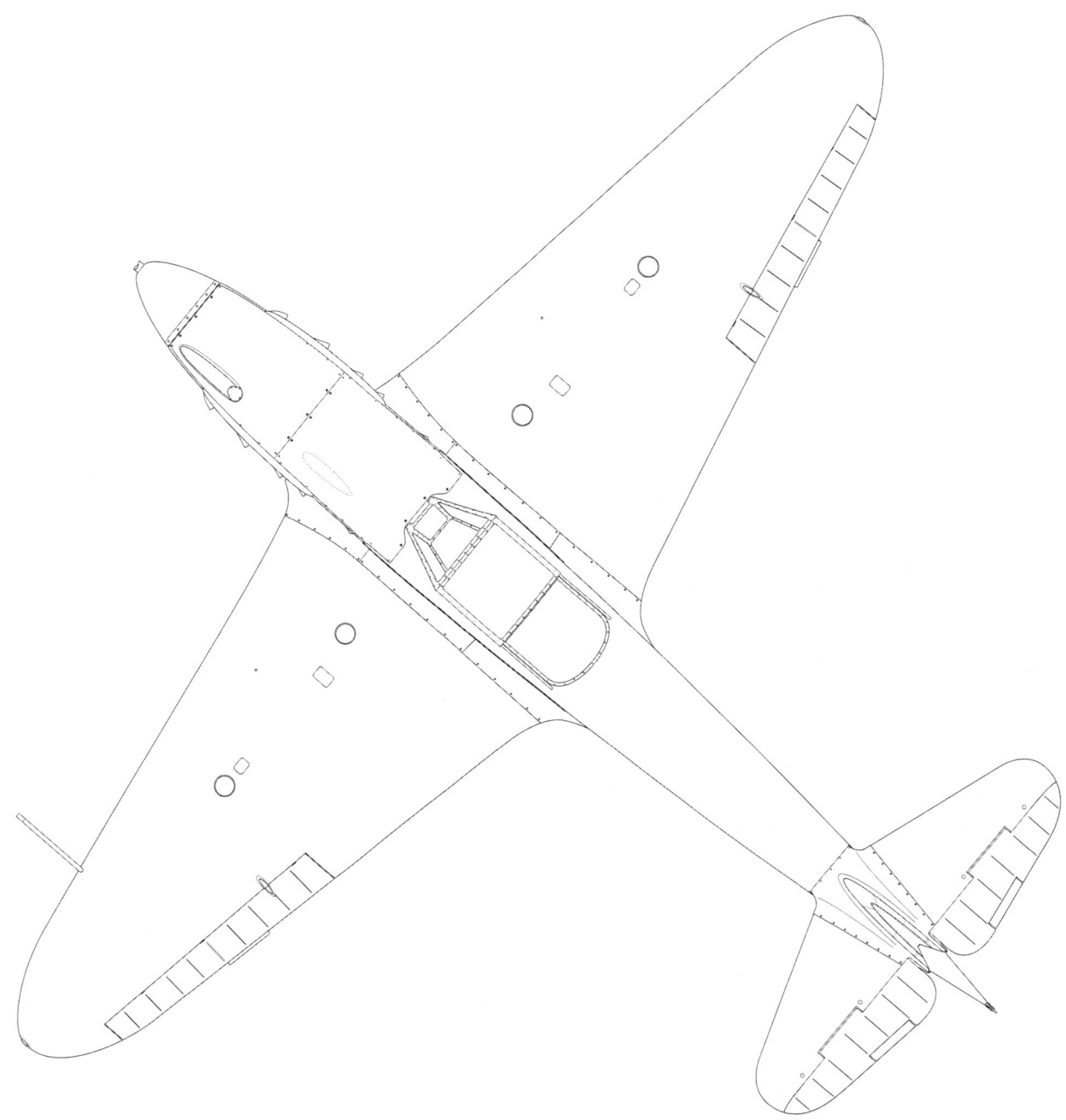

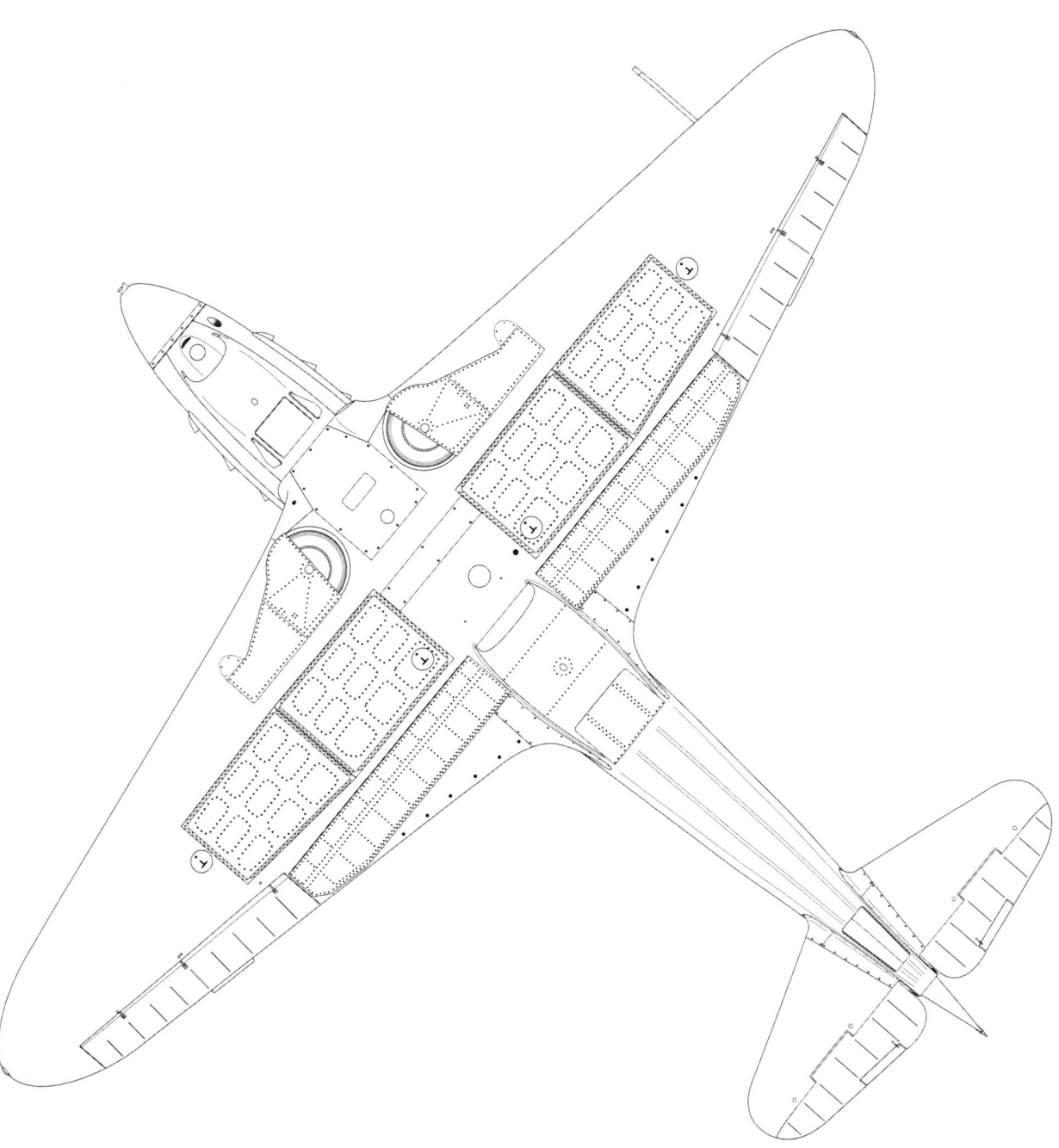

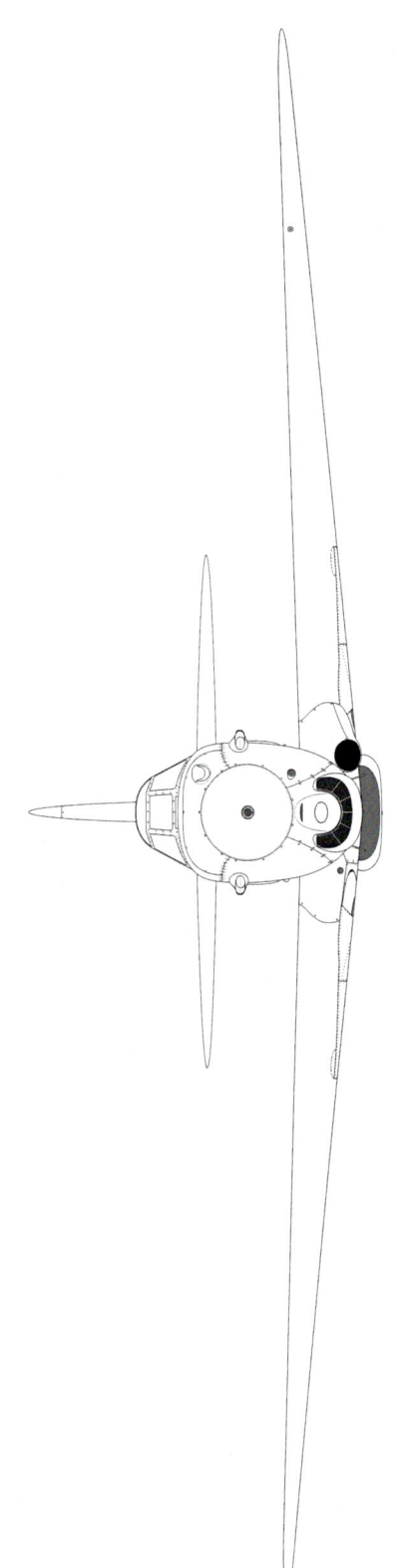

Engine:
- Klimov M-105PF, 1260 hp for take-off & emergency

Armament:
- 1 x 20 mm ShVAK cannon firing through spinner with 150 rounds

Yak-1B M-106, Factory № 292

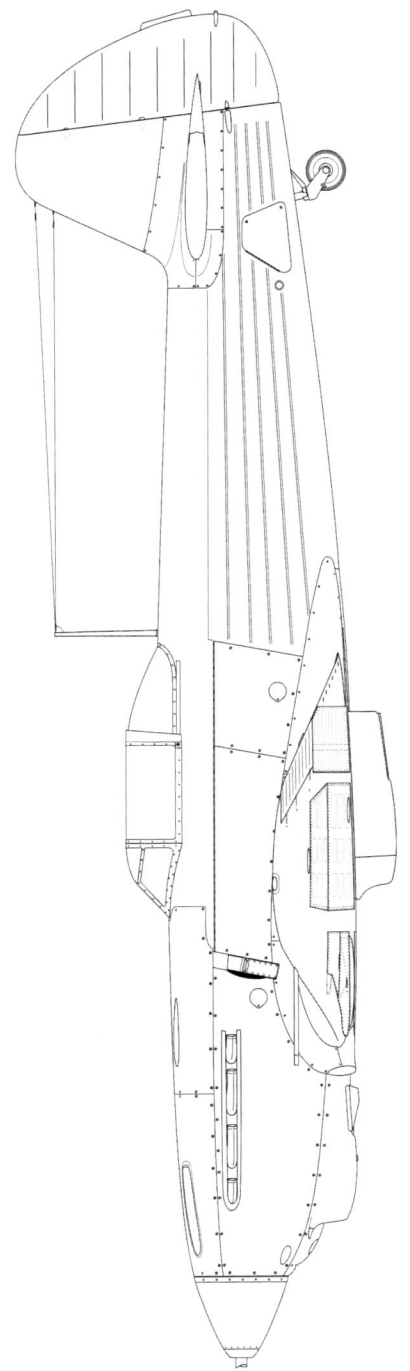

The government had hoped throughout the Yak-1 programme that at some point the more powerful M-106 motor would at last be ready for series manufacture and service use. Alas, that day never arrived. However, and as a result, many Yak-1 examples were fitted with this engine experimentally. Of these, several were actually accepted into service and used by the PVO forces around Moscow.

All of these such aircraft were one-offs, unique prototypes with manifold detail changes. However, during 1944 Factory № 292 was ordered to build a mini series of such M-106 powered examples, these mainly based upon Yak-1B p/n 32-123. Stepanets tells us that at least 32 machines were completed to this standard, but there were other M-106 examples at the same time, and these cannot be assumed to have identical details to the main group (indeed, even the main run show small permutations).

The drawing above shows a common appearance for the "32-123" batch. New exhaust stacks, a new spinner, fixed tail wheel and Yak-7 type radiator make up the main modifications to these aircraft. In most other respects they were identical to a mature (post Series 111) Yak-1B. Many of these aircraft featured a large "M-106" stencil (in red) on the engine cowling.

Glossary & Abbreviations

AII Aviation purpose external cellulose lacquers in use from 1936

AMT and **AGT** Aviation purpose external alkyd lacquers developed at the end of 1941; *M* indicating a **matte** finish and *G* a **gloss** finish

Aviapolk An earlier type of Aviation Regiment, often of mixed composition, usually seen in Naval service at the start of the war

Eskadrilya A Squadron, usually 12-15 aircraft in size

Etalon An individual aircraft built to the standard intended for subsequent mass production

GPW Great Patriotic War, usually refers to the 2nd World War against Nazi Germany, but can be used to refer to the Napoleonic War of 1812

HSU Hero of the Soviet Union, *The Gold Star* medal

IAD (*Istrebitel'nii Aviadiviziya*) Fighter Air Division, usually comprising four to six Regiments

IAK (*Istrebitel'nii Aviakorpus*) Fighter Air Corps, usually comprising three to five Divisions

IAP (*Istrebitel'nii Aviapolk*) Fighter Air Regiment, usually comprising three to four Squadrons

LII (*Letno-Islyedovatel'skii Institut*) Flight Research Institute

NIPAV The Scientific Institute for Testing Aviation Armament

NKAP or Narkomaviaprom (*Narodnii Kommisariat Aviatsionoi Promishlinosti*) People's Commissariat for the Aircraft Industry

NII VVS (*Nauchno-Ispitatel'nii Institut Voyenno-Vozdushikh Sili*) Scientific Test Institute of the Army Air Forces

MAP (*Ministerstvo Aviatsionnaya Promishlinost'*) Ministry of the Aviation Industry; replaced the NKAP [which, see] after the war

Massovii Literally, "mass produced"; a term used widely to describe mature production versions or examples

Oblegchenyi Lightened, often abbreviated as "*obl*"

OKB (*Opitnoe Konstruktorskoe Byuro*) Experimental Design Bureau

P/N Production Number, also given frequently in Russian sources as **Factory Number**; the terms are synonymous

Polk (*Aviapolk*) Regiment (Aviation Regiment)

PVO The Air Defence Forces of the Red Army

Razvedchik Reconnaissance

Taran A ramming attack

TASS (*Telegrafnoe Argenstvo Sovetskogo Soyuza*) Telegraph Agency of the Soviet Union

Tekcnichesoe Opisanie Technical Manual

UA (*s ulyushennoy aehrodinamikoi*) 'With Improved Aerodynamics'

UTI (*Uchebno-trenirovannii istrebitel'*) Fighter-Trainer Aircraft

UVVS (*Upravlenie Voyenno-Vozdushnikh Sili*) Directorate of the Air Forces

VVS (*Voyenno-Vozdushne Sili*) Army Air Forces

VVS VMF (*Voyenno-Vozdushne Sili Voenno-Morskogo Flota*) Naval Air Forces

Cyrillic Transliteration Method

The Russian to English transliteration system employed in the Profile & Scale series.

А	Б	В	Г	Д	Е	Ё	Ж	З	И	Й	К	Л	М	Н	О	П
A	B	V	G	D	E	E	Zh	Z	I	I	K	L	M	N	O	P

Р	С	Т	У	Ф	Х	Ц	Ч	Ш	Щ	Ь	Ы	Ъ	Э	Ю	Я
R	S	T	U	F	Kh	Ts	Ch	Sh	Sh	'	Y	'	Eh	Yu	Ya

Recommended Reading

Istrebiteli Yak-- Perioda Velikoi Otchestvennoi Voiny [Mashinostronie Press] A. T. Stepanets 1992 [ISBN 5-217-01192-0]

Pervyi Yak (**Перый Як**) [Lyubimaya Kniga] Sergei Kuznetsov 1995 [ISBN 5-7656-0001-8]

Yak-1 -- Our Best Fighter of 1941 [Eksmo] Sergei Kuznetsov 2010 [ISBN 978-5-699-39410-4]

Monographie Lotnicze № 46 Jak-1, Jak-3 [AJ-Press] Robert Bock 1998 [ISBN 83-86209-90-2]

Yakovlev's Piston-Engined Fighters [Midland Publishing] Efim Gordon, Dmitri Khazanov [ISBN 1 85780 140 7]

Russian Piston Aero Engines [Crowood Press Ltd] Vladimir Kotelnikov 2005 [ISBN 1 86126 702 9]

The History of Aircraft Construction in the USSR, Vols. 1 and 2 [Mashinostroenie Publication] V.B. Shavrov 1978 [Ш 31808-189]

Chronology of Aviation Production in the USSR, 8th Edition Ivan Rodinov 2002-2018

Appendix I Yak-1 Colouration and Camouflage

The discussion of Yak-1 colouration-- and indeed of all Soviet VVS colouration during the Great Patriotic War-- remains an on going process. Much of this work is visible on the author's web site [www.redbanner.co.uk], and readers may follow the QR code links to these pages. However, having said that, a good deal of new material has surfaced in the last decade regarding Yak fighters, specifically, and several new airframes have been examined by the author yielding more physical examples of period lacquer.

The author would like to point out two immediate facts: 1) That all of these new samples are utterly in agreement with the many physical samples of VVS paint collected hitherto; 2) That all of the new documentary evidence which has surfaced is also in agreement with the physical evidence gathered over the years. A third qualification must be added, in that while documentary evidence is important and extremely helpful, *one cannot determine the appearance of period aviation lacquer without recovering and analysing physical samples of paint.*

The Two Paint Systems

During the summer of 1941 the Government decided to produce a new type of aviation use lacquer known as the AMT type. These new finishes were capable of application to un-primed surfaces, and the Government was convinced that this property would assist both in production and field maintenance. These new AMT finishes were meant to replace all existing lacquers, and of these the AII type finishes were used primarily on the Yak-1 (albeit Factory № 301 did use some AEh-15 Green paint as well). A new factory had to be built to produce these new paints (№ 30 *Aehrolak*, in Moscow), and thus it is no surprise that the initial batches of the finish did not physically materialise until the autumn of 1941.

Quite prudently, the Government decided to introduce these new and unproven finishes at a single aviation factory, who in turn would work with the № 30 plant to develop and refine the lacquers. The chosen facility was Factory № 21 at Gor'ki, home of the Lavochkin OKB. The LaGG-3 fighter manufactured at this facility was the first aircraft finished in these paints, just before the switch to winter white colouration in November. During the spring of 1942 temperate camouflage resumed at Gor'ki making use of AMT-4/-6/-7 lacquers, and by the summer these paints were considered to be successful and distribution began henceforth to other aviation facilities, and to various Army maintenance units in the field.

Therefore, one may see that no AMT type lacquers existed at Factory № 292 prior to the summer of 1942. We should not see any cases of factory camouflage at Saratov before this date using AMT finishes, and indeed this is exactly what the archaeological record demonstrates. I-26 and Yak-1 aircraft built at Factory № 292 used AII type lacquers up to this time. The base finish for the upper surface was two coats of AII Green followed by one coat of AII Black in a disruptive pattern, then two coats of AII Light Blue for the undersurfaces. This finish arrangement is specified comprehensively in NKAP Order № 417ss (amending Resolution KO N 53ss), which also explains why no specific mention is

VVS Colour Chips   VVS Colour Discussion

made of lacquer AII Green, in that *multiple green paints were in use at the time for aircraft finishing*. These details are further reinforced by the official 1942 manual, "Provisional Guide for Yak-1 Aircraft Repair" [Временное руководство по ремонту самолетов Як-1], which instructs units in field repair operations to use AMT-4 Green and AMT-6 Black for the upper surfaces, but to continue to employ AII Light Blue on the undersurfaces as, "...the aircraft were finished [thus] at the factory".

Some other curiosities may be observed in these documents. The original Resolution KO N 53ss suggested the use of lacquer "AM-26" Black for upper surface camouflage. However, this is not the correct nomenclature for any actual VVS paint; there was no type "AM-". When this document was produced (29 April) the effective instructions for the manufacture of the new lacquers (417ss) had not yet been created, and presumably this idea in fact referred to the eventual paints AMT-6 or A-26m Black. Furthermore, KO N 53ss resolved that all aircraft undersurfaces were to be finished with a *light grey* colour, something which never came to pass. Six upper surface colours were mooted for the new (AMT) lacquer system, but in the autumn only Green, Black and Blue were manufactured. AMT-1 was eventually seen (in 1943), but there is no record of what -2, -3 and -5 were meant to be.

In terms of the actual appearance of these various colours, we must look to the physical record of surviving paint samples. The very newest evidence collected with respect to the Yak-1 aircraft has come from airframes 13-42, 11-13, 39-78 and 15-18. All samples collected are in perfect agreement, both with regards to each other, and also with respect to the newly unearthed documentary evidence. To the right are a set of digital, and now printed, reproduction colour chips. These *cannot* replicate the true physical appearance of the colours, as such reproduction technology does not exist either in the digital nor printing worlds. These are approximations, for comparison only.

These chips may be compared to the actual samples collected from the various aircraft. Bear in mind, of course, that these samples are highly worn and corroded, and incompetently photographed by the author. They do not perfectly match their 'as new' appearance, obviously. However, their *relative appearance* may be compared to the appearance of these same paints on period photography. AMT-4 Green is darker than AII Green; AMT-7 Blue is lighter than AII Light Blue; and so on.

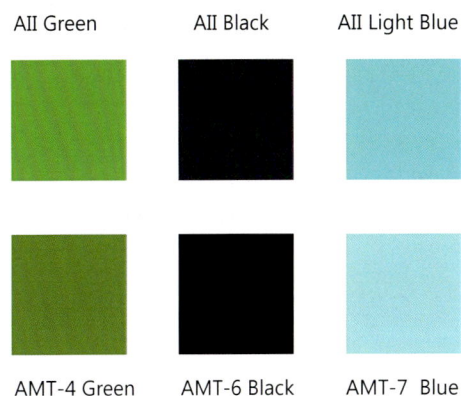

| AII Green | AII Black | AII Light Blue |
| AMT-4 Green | AMT-6 Black | AMT-7 Blue |

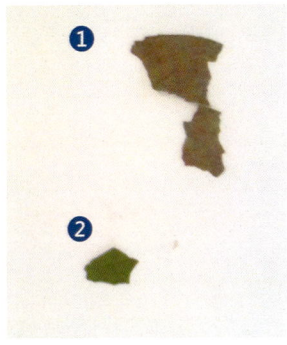

❶ AII Green sample from the wing root (highly worn, exposed to elements) of 13-42.
❷ AMT-4 sample from the wing root ejection slot (less exposed / worn) of a Yak-7B.

The port wing root fairing of 13-42 next to the starboard unit from a Yak-7B finished with AMT paints (alas, p/n currently unknown). The two greens are evidently different to the naked eye, even upon casual inspection.

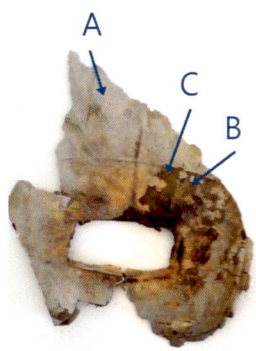

Rudder fabric from 15-18. This confirms the official finishing instructions exactly: two coats of AIN clear dope; one coat of AII Aluminium (A); two coats of AII Green (B); then a field application of two coats of AMT-4 (C).

AII and AMT paints in the same image on Russian monochromatic film.

AII and AMT paints on Yak-7s (displayed at Rechlin) *via* German monochromatic film.

One last colour matter must be addressed. Many fine researchers have put forward the idea that VVS aircraft were painted with supposed paints A-18F Blue and A-19F Green prior to the introduction of AMT finishes (especially during 1940-41). This author does not deny that such a recommendation was made. HOWEVER, he also asks, "Where are these paints"? The A- series primers are extremely well known. Many samples have been collected by the author, and there are many more surviving extant examples besides. The suffix "F" also tells us that the paints in question were alcohol solving permutations of the A- family primers. Thus we have specifically internal use primers with an alcohol solvent alledgedly for use on aircraft external surfaces?

103

The author simply cannot see that such a thing was likely, suggested by the Government or not. Many, many such recommendations were put forward by the Government at this time regarding all manner of things related to aviation which were not put into practice, often for reasons of incompetence. This instruction would join that group. To employ a primer as a surface finish-- let alone one which was alcohol soluble in the famously harsh Russian weather conditions-- for military aircraft would result in cataclysmic failure. The photographic record would be absolutely full of aircraft with their surface finish peeling away, or indeed gone altogether. Such scenes of paint failure are nowhere to be found. Moreover, no such physical sample of these paints has ever been located, and

no external paint sample has ever been collected from any authentic airframe featuring an alcohol solving external lacquer of any description, and certainly not an A- series primer.

Until such time as actual examples of a paint are found (and examined) which could in fact be A-18 or -19F lacquer, we simply cannot consider these claims seriously. The pre-AMT green and blue paint used on Soviet aircraft at the time are very well known, always identical in appearance and chemistry and span the entire industry, from Polikarpov to Petlyakov. These paints cannot be the result of a specific recommendation made to Factory № 292 at Saratov. And lastly, they simply are not A-family primers.

Winter White Finish

A brief word regarding the use of MK-7 White on the Yak-1 is in order. This lacquer was not unusual in terms of its colour, which was simply *white*, but rather with respect to its surface finish. MK-7 featured a very matte surface, and this was seen to be ideal for military use. Indeed, the finish was very dull, but in the case of MK family paints (the same problem was encountered with night finish MK-6 later) this dull sheen was achieved by means of a very rough surface. In fact, the surface was so irregular that it resulted in rather pronounced aerodynamic drag, something which came as a particularly rude shock to the pilots of the VVS.

Worse still, this family of aviation paint turned out to be inadequate in terms of its adherent quality, as well. MK-7 was supposed to be applied to the already painted surface of aircraft at the factory or in the field. This means that the finish should have adhered to either cellulose or alkyd paint equally, a goal which, realistically, would have been exceedingly challenging, even in the modern day with the use of polyurethane lacquers. In the event, MK finish did not stick well to either surface, and neither as well to unpainted surfaces, failing comprehensively in this regard. As a result of this unhappy situation, the majority of cases of 'removed' winter finish observed during 1941-42 were not likely deliberate. In fact, these cases [see Zhidov's "Red 23", for example] usually show the abject failure of MK-7 White to stick to the aircraft's surface, and fell away at times in large sheets.

In an attempt to ease the application process, the Government introduced a version of the paint that could solve in alcohol (MK-7F). This new version was an improvement in terms of being able to be removed, especially under field conditions, but if anything it actually adhered worse than the original formula. The Government suggested that units thin the paint for application, but this solution was not a major improvement,

and by 1943 the majority of the VVS abandoned the finish altogether.

These manifold problems with MK lacquer explain the curious variety of appearances of worn winter finish seen in the photographic record during the winters of 1941-42, and subsequently of 1942-43. Early Yak-1s seen during the first spring (1942) season demonstrate many underlying surface colouration details. Some clearly show two underlying upper surface colours, and thus a full temperate camouflage scheme. Others seem to show a uniform underlying colouration, and this might have been an over-all green application (mostly AII Green), or in case perhaps even ALG-1 primer. One can imagine that, in an attempt to get MK lacquer to stick to the surfaces, the factories might have tried a number of methods of application when using it.

The final use of MK winter paint took place on early Yak-1Bs manufactured at Saratov. These machines were finished with what was described as an 'improved' formulation of MK-7F. The subsequent significant wear visible in the photographic record, followed by the abandonment of the finish, give lie to the accuracy of this claim.

One last note on alcohol solving aircraft finish: it tends to be highly problematic. Certainly A- series primers were more competent in adherence than MK- finishes, but even so all of these paints reacted poorly to the wet and cold conditions in Russia. Had the factories actually used these proposed A-18F and A-19F paints on the external surfaces of aircraft prior to the introduction of AMT, we would have overwhelming evidence of this use in the pictorial record (as well as the physical record). No such evidence exists. The author concludes that the same may be said of these alleged finishes.

Hawker Hurricane Mk IIs finished with *improved* MK-7F lacquer, winter of 1942-43.

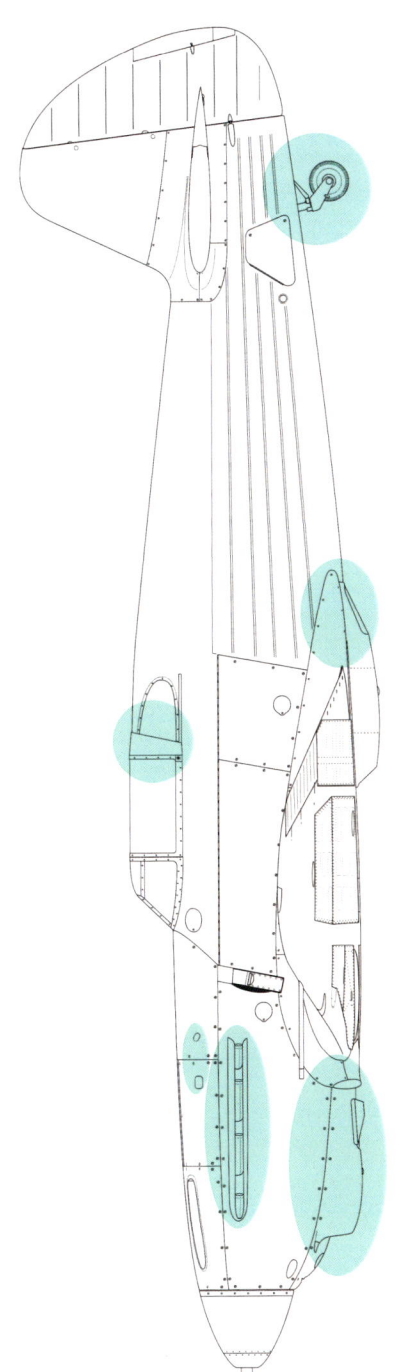

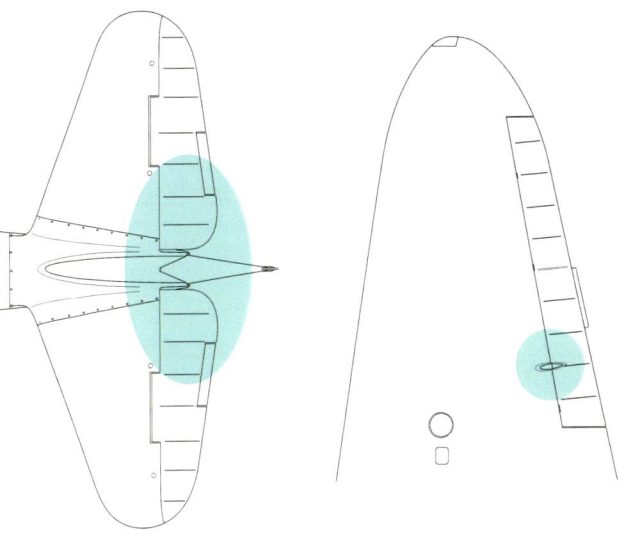

In the quest to improve the Yak-1 family's performance, many individual prototype examples played their part. In these efforts two distinct threads of development could be noted, the first of which was to improve the fighter's systems and configuration. Factory № 115 built Yak-1 10-47 with a cut-down rear fuselage, and this arrangement with Yak-1B style armament was perfected on Saratov's 35-60. The other thread of improvement centred on aerodynamic refinement, and the main airframe used for this purpose was 08-68. This aircraft was rebuilt several times, the work stemming from an intensive series of discussions between the NII VVS, the LII, the NKAP and Yakovlev's OKB. This series of aerodynamic and structural improvements is often referred to as the "UA" (*s ulyushennoy aehrodinamikoi*) project, which was finally realised on the Yak-1B model from Series 111. The main changes and improvements included: new shrouded exhaust stacks; filled gas ports; re-shaped oil cooler and exit flap; fairing on aft sliding canopy; retractable tail wheel; re-shaped starboard wing root intake; modified radiator bath exhaust flap; streamlined aileron hinges; revised elevator at the 'heel' near to the rudder.

Yak-1 № 08-68 at the NII VVS, likely during June 1942. A succession of modifications to the aircraft make it somewhat difficult to date the image precisely, but in this view it looks to still have a fixed tail wheel at least.

Appendix III Yak Fighter Stabiliser Development

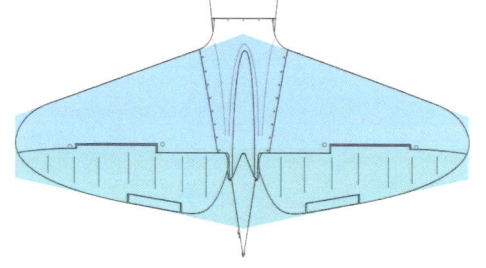

I-26 Prototypes,
I-26 Moscow Production

Published Area Figures

Total Area: 3.05 m2
Stabiliser Area: 1.93 m2
Elevator Area: 1.12 m2

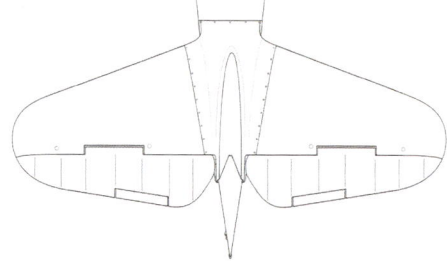

Yak-1,
I-26 Saratov Production

Published Area Figures

Total Area: 3.05 m2
Stabiliser Area: 1.82 m2
Elevator Area: 1.23 m2

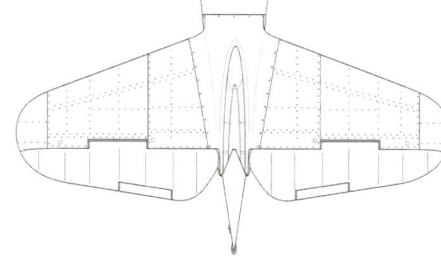

Yak-1 *oblegchennii*
Series 96
Yak-7, Yak-9

Published Area Figures

Total Area: 3.05 m2
Stabiliser Area: 1.82 m2
Elevator Area: 1.23 m2

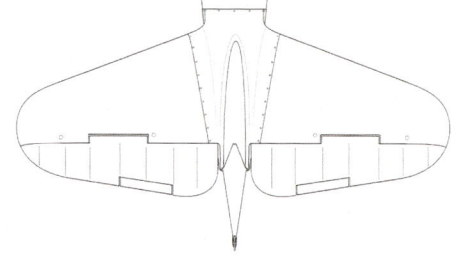

Yak-1B 'UA'
(Series 111)

Published Area Figures

Total Area: 3.05 m2
Stabiliser Area: 1.82 m2
Elevator Area: 1.23 m2

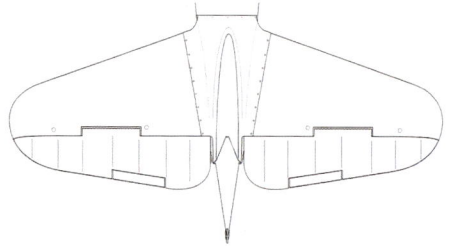

Yak-1M Prototypes,
Yak-1B *oblegchennii*,
Yak-3

Published Area Figures

Total Area: 3.0 m2
Stabiliser Area: 1.77 m2
Elevator Area: 1.23 m2

Appendix IV Yak-1B № 08-110

Yak-1B 08-110 is a much discussed-- and widely argued-- authentic survivor now housed in the Saratov Regional Museum of Local Lore. The current appearance of this machine can be seen in the image, right, and as it appeared when it was moved to its current home, below right. The various odd features of the aircraft have caused many observers to react with horror, and indeed a fair number of aviation enthusiasts regard this exhibit as a gratuitous fake.

Happily, this machine is the actual № 08-110, albeit is has received a number of inauthentic external parts, and is the subject of some remedial re-configuration. The author saw this aircraft when it was in storage at the old Saratov aviation plant on Ordzhonikidze Street back in 1988. At the time, it had been disassembled into its major parts-- wings, fuselage and stabilisers. An M-105 engine was present, but not mounted on the airframe. No propeller or spinner were seen, neither were the control surfaces, and the various fillets (wing root, stabs, etc) were missing.

◄ The wing root fillets, absurd and ill-fitting, certainly look to have come from an Orenburg Yak Warbird, as widely condemned. Why on earth anyone would fit such things to a *Yak-1* defies any understanding, and these units result in a *preposterous* appearance. The oil cooler is not an authentic part-- only a shaped piece of sheet metal-- and there is no exit flap at all. The engine exhaust stacks and the shroud do, however, seem to be Yak-1B type items.

The current paint finish is a dark green and light blue livery using unknown lacquers. As such, the Eremin dedication inscriptions (both sides) are not the same as in the 1940s appearance, but rather an approximation of those.

► Noting these Warbird wing root fillets, speculation has abounded that the wings, themselves, were Orenburg units. However, one may see, right, that the landing gear bay shows a proper wooden Yak wing, and a quick measurement of this item should reveal that it has a correct 10 m span. The empennage fillet is also from a Yak Warbird, and in fact it would appear that so are all of the control surfaces, themselves. The elevators certainly look to be 'Yak-3' style items.

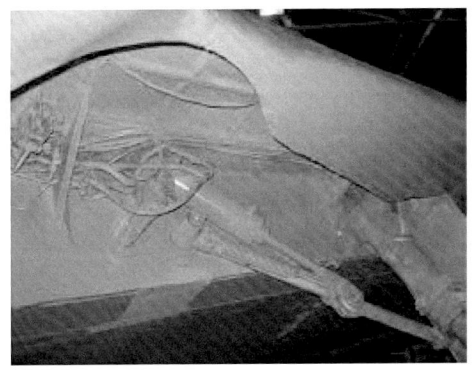

◄ The spinner might be a Yak-3 unit, or taken from a post-war Yak-9P; it is hard to be sure from this view. The forward section of the main body of the lower cowling appears to be genuine, at least back to the oil cooler, and is quite battered and worn. The forward oval intake on the cowling has been closed over.

L - #0382 - 200120 - C110 - 279/216/8 - PB - DID2744652